Social Justice
Begins in the Womb

By: Bryan Kemper

CLAY BRIDGES
COMMUNICATIONS & PUBLISHING

Troy, Ohio

Permissions

Requests for information, copyright permissions, or comments should be addressed to:
Clay Bridges Communications & Publishing, 300 South Ridge Avenue, Troy, Ohio, 45373 or
info@claybridges.com.

Social Justice Begins in the Womb is a Clay Bridges Communications & Publishing publication.

Clay Bridges seeks to provide resources and education to build up people to span life's
circumstances. For speaking, training, or author events, visit www.claybridges.com or contact us at
the information listed above.

Library of Congress Control Number: 2009934485
ISBN: 978-0-9819807-5-1

Printed and Manufactured in the United States of America

Dedication

This book is dedicated to every child who has lost their voice before they could never tell their parents, "I love you." As long as I have a voice and breath, I will Stand True as a voice for you.

Acknowledgements

I have too many people to thank so if you are not listed, please don't take it personally. I am just an old fart who forgets a lot of things.

I know it is cliché to thank God first, but it is cliché for a reason. God should always come first. I know without Christ I could do nothing, be nothing, and achieve nothing. With Christ I can do all things.

I dedicate this to: Carrie, my bride, you still take my breath away. Kimberlee, Abigayle, Madilynn, Jaemison, Atticus, Emmerich, and any future chillins.

Jeremy, Shawn, Emma, Juan, Canadia, Sam, Eric T., Cameron, Alana, Louie, Dan, Megan, Sarah H., Courtney, Jody, Andrew, Cynthia, Kate B., Hannah R., Jake, and the rest of the Stand True family. Pastor Steve, Liam & Bev, Greg & Elisa, the Whites, the Conrads, the Schiedlers, the Mahoneys, Will G., the Boyers, the Ruizes, the Kriegs, Reese, the AZ crew, Pastor Bob, the Kribs, the Federicos, Pastor Jackson, and everyone else my forty-two-year-old brain forgot.

One Truth (RIP), Ephraim, The Love Alliance, The Survivors, Clay Bridges, Alliance Defense Fund, The Pro-life Action League, Youth Defence, Noneunderground, Generations for Life, Thorn, Enthos, American Life League, Youth For Life Australia, Abort73, Operation Rescue, Rock For Life, Students for Life of America, Generation Life, Priests for Life, Cornerstone Festival, Creation Festival, Soul Festival, Purple Door Festival, Alive Festival, Tom Fest, Lifest, Tae Ryu Do, and Night Sky Cafe.

Bradley Hathaway, Kutless, Ilia, Family Force Five, Spoken, Superchick, POD, Casting Crowns, Mewithoutyou, Alove for Enemies, Supertones, Five Iron Frenzy, John Reuben, Fireflight, Pillar, Lecland, NIV, Overcome, Focused, Precious Death, Jordan, Narcissus, The Crucified, and all the bands who have not been afraid of being a voice.

Table of Contents

Section Four: *Reflections on God*

Introduction

Social justice is all the rage right now. So many different social justice organizations are popping up everywhere, it is hard to keep track. I am not saying this in a negative way; I think it is awesome that people want to take action and do something to love those in need.

I want to point out two things I have noticed two things about this social justice trend. The first is most social justice organizations we see leave out the plight of the children in the womb who are facing death everyday. For too many people, the social justice timeline begins at birth—when it should start at the beginning of life. So many groups want to save children's lives but don't include the children who are being killed every day by abortion. Many other people buy the cool T-shirt, proclaiming their stance on an issue, and then their action ends.

I think it is great that so many kids want to buy a T-shirt to help spread an important message and support a cause. I only wish it would go further than just a cool T-shirt. It is easy just to wear a shirt with a message; the hard part is living out that message.

Cutting, starvation, human trafficking, AIDS, and child labor are all tragedies that should deeply concern all of us.

Each of these issues deserves our prayers and action. While all of these causes are popular to be involved with, the killing of innocent children in the womb is often overlooked or ignored. If you are willing to take a stand against the inhumanity of human trafficking or child labor, you should also be willing to take a stand against the killing of almost 4,000 innocent children every day through abortion.

The social justice mission must begin in the womb.

Foreword
by eric samuel timm

As I sit here thinking of my future I'm perplexed.
I'm wondering what will become of this world I'm in.
Right now, it sure seems dark. Dark enough to even hide.
In the long run of life I have only been here for a short while,
and yet I have heard so much.
I've listened to arguments, shouting, and the eerie silence
that reeks of decision.
Decision rooted in information, convictions, and ideals.
I wish I could provide more information for some, for that is the
only heart they listen to. There also seems to be sides.
There also seems to be a choice:
A choice of which perspective to take.
All these voices are speaking at once.
Some voices carry, they echo. These voices pierce steel ears.
They challenge both perspectives and ring the sound of hope.
I heard this one guy, Bryan, who is this type of voice.
He was saying that God told me once
that I was going to be and now I am.
I think he thinks I have an idea that is locked
inside my brain that will change the world.
Something new that I know is not yet discovered, I can feel it.
Some that need to be freed; I can free them.
There is hope that has not been given that I have.
I have a purpose, a reason. But yet I'm unborn.

Eric Samuel Timm is part artist, speaker, author, and all passion—this is what gives Rev.
Timm relevance in today's schools and universities As he speaks, paints and performs,
Eric captivates his audiences with his unique style and unforgettable one-of-a-kind live
art performances. His mission is to paint and perform live the messages of truth, hope,
and love—and inspire you to create with purpose. He is sought after for his ability to
present God's truth in ways that connect both with the Church and to a person whom is
on the fringe of faith. Eric stirs up what lays dormant and leaves his audiences inspired.
When he speaks, they'll listen—when he paints, you will see art differently. Eric resides
north of Minneapolis, Minnesota with his wife Danielle and son Xavier.

Opening
I'm Bryan Kemper

While the title may sound narcissistic, it is actually a joke that has turned into a game we play every summer on the Christian music festival circuit. "I'm Bryan Kemper" has gotten my friends and I backstage, to the front of five-hour lines, free food, and so much more each summer. The funny part is that I usually have backstage access anyway; it is just more fun to hide my pass and just say "I'm Bryan Kemper."

In 1993 I had three strong passions in life: Jesus, music, and life. I spent most of my free time either at concerts or pro-life events. The first used the "I'm Bryan Kemper" line, I did it as a joke. I'd forgotten my pass to get backstage, and when I needed to get backstage, I just said, "I'm Bryan Kemper." It was more about attitude than the words, but they let me backstage. Now, it's a standing line that many of my friends, both male and female have used to get backstage.

While I was heavily involved with my passions, I was still spending most of my time working dead end jobs and hating every minute of it. In the fall of 1993 I was undercover inside of an abortion mill as part of what pro-lifers called a "truth team" putting pro-life literature inside magazines. That day changed my life forever.

We entered the abortion mill, and my truth team partner asked for a pregnancy test as I sat down in the lobby. She went to the back room and distributed literature as I did so in the lobby. She was taking way too long, so I approached the counter to ask about her. That is when the door behind the counter opened. I stood in shock as I realized I was staring into the abortion room and saw a young teenage girl on her back with tears pouring out of her eyes. I watched the doctor's hands reach down to start the abortion. I witnessed a human person being killed right in front of me, and a young woman probably emotionally damaged for life.

I went home that night and cried out to God, asking what I could do to stop this holocaust.

I heard a voice, I am not sure where it came from, but I heard it say, "Bryan, save my children." I saw a picture in my head of hundreds of thousands of young people taking a stand for life. That was the birth of Rock for Life, and what has become the youth pro-life movement in America.

I spent the next ten years running Rock for Life and building a youth pro-life movement by combining two of my greatest passions: music and pro-life. I wanted to give youth a movement they could take ownership of and call their own. I wanted to give them tools and materials that were relevant to them and their generation.

In 2003, after ten years, I left Rock for Life and started a new organization called Stand True. I wanted to focus more on a Christ-centered, pro-life approach and develop more tools and activities for young people to get involved in. Stand True was formed to educate, activate, and equip this generation to take a stand for Christ and human life.

At Stand True we have developed a hugely successful pro-life clothing and accessory line. We have rethought message clothing as we produce T-shirts that are more artistic and thought provoking rather then screaming in your face and judgmental.

We have developed pro-life events like the Pro-life Day of Silent Solidarity, which students from more than 48,000 campuses in 25 countries participated in last year, and we have heard stories of (at least) 57 high school girls canceling abortion appointments as a result of the events.

We have developed a line of educational materials including Life Cards, pro-life postcards with amazing art and graphics, literature, and much more.

Our web sites—a list of which you can find on the back cover of this book—provide students with great resources for doing pro-life projects in school as well as keeping them informed of pro-life events and activities.

Over the past twenty years I have been writing poetry and commentaries about pro-life and faith. I have collected some of my favorites and put them together to share with you here in this collection.

My hope is that this book will inspire you to write your own stories and lend your voice to the cause for the babies.

My hope is that you will use the journal section in the back and then send your thoughts to Stand True either by mail, through our Facebook fan page, or email.

section one

pro-life commentaries

The Other Night

The other night I had a dream.
I dreamt I was in Hell.
It wasn't like you think,
It was sort of like this Earth.
I remember walking down the street,
Wandering about.
I came upon a poor man,
Shivering in the street.
His feet were bare,
His clothes were torn,
Tangles in his hair.
He looked as if
He'd been beaten up,
More than a time or two.
His stench was heavy in the air,
I had to hold my breath.

As I turned away,
A scream pierced my ear.
The fragile woman laying there,
Unable to move at all.
As he ripped at her clothes,
I could not stand to watch.
He took from her what was not his,
With no Remorse at all.
I had to leave,
I could not stand to watch.
I started to feel her pain.

Around the corner,
I saw a girl.
She smelled of cheap perfume.
She smiled at me,

And with a wink,
Said all there was to say.
Thirteen, maybe fourteen,
That's as old as she could be.
Her parents must be worried:
Where could their daughter be?

Next I stumbled upon a child,
His body, battered and bruised.
I stood in shock
As I looked up,
He fell to the hands
Of his own father.

How much more
Can I take
Of these morbid scenes of Hell?

Up in the distance,
I see a line,
Forming at a door.
Out the back came a man,
Carrying a garbage bag.
In they filed
To add to the pile
Of America's disgrace.

All of a sudden, I tripped and fell,
I was in great pain.
But, wait a minute!
This was a dream.
How could I feel this pain?

A dream indeed,
No, not at all.
This is our very own world.

13

With all this wealth
In the world,
Why can't we feed the poor?
When we see someone
Is in distress,
Why can't we call for help?
Why won't someone do something
About parents who hurt their kids?
And about this slaughter
Of pre-born babies,
Why won't someone speak out?

Wait a minute!
What am I saying?
How can I be so blind?
Why leave it up
To someone else?
What makes me so special?
Oh God, Oh God,
Please have mercy!
Have mercy on my soul.
This was not a dream,
This was not Hell,
This is the real world.

Next time I walk
Down the these streets
And see these morbid sights,
Will I make an effort
To make a difference
In someone else's life?
The answer came in a dream,
A dream I had last night.
As I passed all those people,
The face I saw was Christ' s.

1 - I am Protesting, Protesting

If you have ever seen the movie PCU (Politically Correct University), you will understand what I mean by "protesting, protesting." The movie makes fun of people who live to protest; they find something wrong with everything and protest it to get their points across.

A Stand True team member praying outside the abortion mill, Kettering, Ohio, Summer 2008

I used to be a major protester. I would drop everything for a good protest. I have been to jail several times, been sued by Janet Reno twice, and am considered a hate criminal by the republic of Canada. I used to have protest signs in my vehicle at all times, and my kids would love to "go hold signs." I think there is definitely a time and place for protesting. Look at the Civil Rights Movement: it proved that protesting can work, and in big ways.

Over the years, I have done most of my protesting at abortion clinics. I used to hold giant bloody signs and yell at the people going into the clinics. I would yell, "Shame on you for killing your baby," or "Real men don't have their babies murdered." I was always ready with a remark to people walking into the clinic, but never ready to listen to them. I was more worried about proving my point, so much so that many times I never gave them a chance to ask for help.

Now, I want to make it clear that, as a pro-life activist, I believe strongly in going to abortion clinics. In fact, Stand True holds prayer vigils at abortion mills every January during the *March for Life* weekend. However, we will not be holding giant signs and yelling.

I have been a pro-life activist for over twelve years and have seen many different methods of outreach at abortion clinics.

What I know works better than any other method is prayer and sidewalk counseling.

Why are pro-lifers there in the first place? Is it to stop someone from having an abortion? I hope that is not the only reason we are there.

The women entering the clinic are not just stopping in for an abortion like it was a trip to the grocery store. Most of the women that go into these clinics are scared, lonely, and don't know where else to turn. They believe abortion is their only option, and no one will help them. They believe abortion is their only hope.

I have seen this for many years. I have talked to hundreds of men and women outside of abortion clinics and heard them talk about how this was the only way. They believed there was no one to help them. I have heard how scared they are and how hurt they are because they think no one cares. I have watched as parents forcibly escorted their daughter into a clinic while she bawled her eyes out. I have seen young girls walk out doubled over in pain as their boyfriends just sit in the car smoking, not even willing to get out and open the door.

I have seen anti-abortion protesters scream and yell as they wave their signs in these girls' faces and call them horrible names. I have watched these girls just close up and walk right in ignoring the hatred being spewed at them. We need to be there to offer hope and love for these girls.

Imagine yourself as a woman, walking to an abortion clinic. You'd probably be scared out of your mind. On one side of the street you see people with giant bloody signs yelling and telling you not to murder your baby. On the other side, you see someone smiling and asking if you are OK. Asking if there anything they can do to help you. Offering you information about a free help center that is willing to help you and your baby. To which side would you go?

These women don't need to be protested against; *they need to be loved*. They don't need a lecture; they need someone to talk to them, and listen to them, and be there for them. They need to know that we care about them just as much as we care about their baby.

If pro-lifers scare them off and they don't have an abortion, then we've won—but only partially.

What happens a year later when they are in the same situation again? What happens to that baby in a few years when he or she grows up in the same environment?

We need to be there to offer women hope, not just scare them off. We need to be there to listen to them and share Christ with them. We need to be praying for their hearts to change, not just their minds.

I encourage you to go to an abortion mill. If you are not able to talk to the men or women going in, then pray for them. Pray that God will put someone into their lives who can show them His love and share Christ's hope.

Now, don't think I am saying there is not a time and place for protests or the use of graphic photos. I think there is a time and place. Protesting abortion is something I can agree we all should do.

But protesting the women seeking abortion is not something we should do at all.

2 - Words and Reactions

I'm often asked what people should say to a woman who is considering abortion. I wish there was a magic answer I could give that would help change the mind of every woman thinking about aborting her baby. Sadly, there is not.

The only way even to begin to answer this question is to address what not to say.

I have stood outside abortion mills for over thirteen years praying, protesting, and have even been arrested many times for praying in front of the doors. I have watched thousands of women walk into abortion mills and seen many different approaches by pro-lifers trying to save the babies.

Scripture reading outside the abortion mill,
Kettering, Ohio, Summer 2007

The first mistake I see is anger. Pro-lifers can become so angry about abortion that they sometimes take it out on women and just scare them *into* the abortion mill. I have heard people call women "murderers, whores, Jezebels, devil worshipers," and so much more. I have seen anti-abortion protesters so angry that they actually spit while they scream at people.

I have never once seen this kind of behavior convince a woman to change her mind.

I admit that in the early years I screamed and waved signs in people's faces. I let the frustration get to me as I watched many young girls being taken in to the abortion mill, often by their parents or boyfriends. I would see their boyfriends leaving, going to get food, sitting in the parking lot, or smoking while their child was being killed inside the building. I let frustration get to me and began to rely on myself for results instead of relying on God.

I want to make it clear that not all people who go to abortion mills to minister and pray act like this.

At Stand True, we encourage people to go to the abortion mills for prayer and witnessing. There are highly effective ways of reaching women and helping them to make the right decision.

When a woman goes to an abortion mill, she is usually scared and frustrated. She believes she has no other option than abortion, and no one can help her.

Girls do not need someone yelling at them and telling them how evil they are. They need someone to love them and let them know how precious they are in God's eyes. They need some-one to address their needs, not just the baby's needs. They need someone to approach them in the same way Christ would ap-proach someone who was hurting and scared and about to make a huge mistake.

The first thing we tell people if they are going to try to talk to girls entering abortion mills is not to hold a sign or wear pro-life messages on their shirts. We tell them that they should appear very friendly so they won't immediately scare the women away. We believe the first words to a woman entering the mill should be geared towards her and how she is doing, not just about the baby. Let her know you care about her.

The most powerful thing you can do when going to the abor-tion mill is pray. Nothing is more effective than prayer. When we go to our local abortion mill we spend the first hour as a group reading the Bible out loud, not shouting, but just reading out loud the Word of God. We then walk around the building praying for the women, the doctor, the nurses, the escorts, and every-one involved. We also look for opportunities to be a witness for Christ and share—not only with the women going in—but with the escorts and whoever else may be around. We do not call them names or condemn them to hell. We share Christ's love with them.

These ideas and principles are not just for the abortion mill, but for our everyday life when we run into challenging situations like this.

I recently read an article about a young girl at a Catholic school who got pregnant. She was told she could not walk the stage at her graduation, while the young man was allowed to. Not only was this total hypocrisy, it was a dangerous way to treat a young girl. It is exactly that kind of reaction and treatment of girls that drives them to abortion.

Our words, especially our first words to a girl who gets pregnant, can determine the path she takes and be the difference between life and death. As a father of three daughters, I wonder how I would react if one of my daughters came home one day and told me she was pregnant. What would I say? Would I blow up and lose my temper? Or would I love her no matter what mistake she had made?

When we go to God in prayer and confess our sins, do you think He screams and yells and has a huge fit? I don't think so. Do you think He yells at us and tells us how horrible we are, and how much of a disgrace we are to the family? I don't think so. When we go to Him, He is faithful to love and forgive us. I pray that I never have to go through this with my daughters, but if I do, I pray that my first words to her would be words of love.

Yes, we believe abortion is the act of killing a human person and should never be permitted. Yes, we believe abortion is a sin and is detestable in God's eyes. Yes, we believe we need to stand up against this evil and be there to help people keep from making such a tragic and horrific mistake. But more importantly than all of that, we believe those people need Christ, and we need to love them as Christ would.

"If we confess our sins, He is faithful and just to forgive us our sins and to cleanse us from all unrighteousness" (1 John 1:9, NIV).

3 - Everyday Pro-life

When I speak to an audience, I often say that pro-life is so much more than just anti-abortion.

Being pro-life is not a political stance or even just a stance against the procedure of abortion. I believe being pro-life is a personhood issue, and, even more, a God-issue.

I believe God is the creator of every single human person and has given every human person a soul. That is why I am pro-life.

My pro-life stance does not stop when that child is born; *that is merely the beginning.* My pro-life stand does not stop at their physical life, but also includes their soul. Being pro-life to me means loving more than just the baby, but also loving the woman, the abortion doctor, the nurses, and the clinic escorts. It means loving my neighbor as myself, and that means loving my fellow human person.

At Stand True, we believe that doing pro-life work does not end at stopping abortion, but really begins there. Pro-life work also includes providing for women who choose to keep their children, as well as providing healing ministry for those who have already had an abortion. We don't just want to see women change their minds about abortion, we want to see their hearts changed and see them come to Christ. We don't want just to see the doctors stop killing babies; we want to see them come Christ and seek His forgiveness.

We look around and see so many things we can do that are pro-life.

Recently, we were talking to a clinic escort in Richmond, Virginia, and I was sharing with her my testimony. I talked to her about the rough upbringing I had, and the strange, often horrific journeys I have taken in this life. I shared with her how finding the hope I have found in Christ has changed my life and brought me to where I am today.

She then shared with me how a large group of homeless people gather in a local park to be fed by a group on Sunday nights. Our pro-life group talked about this and believed this would be a great pro-life thing to do. We made plans to go and help the following week.

The tour team covered in mud after pushing the Stand True van out of the mud, Alive Festival, Ohio, Summer 2006

That next Sunday night, we got in our van with a bunch of fruit we had bought and headed to Richmond to help out. From the moment we got there, I could tell the people serving there were uneasy about our presence. Many of them were also people that worked as escorts at the local abortion mill. We told them we wanted to make a donation every month to help them feed people and would come down twice a month to help serve.

A few days later, I received a phone call from one of the group and was told that we were not welcome to help anymore. I tried to talk to her, but it was useless. Unfortunately this group decided that because we were pro-life we were not welcome to feed the homeless with them. (I wonder how the homeless would feel about this.)

I can't tell you how many times pro-abortion activists have asked me if I ever do anything for people who are already born. The door closed this time in Richmond. Fortunately, we have found many other opportunities to work in homeless ministry.

We may not be welcome at that park in Richmond, but that shouldn't and won't stop us from doing what we feel is important. We looked around and found a place in Fredericksburg, Virginia that feeds the homeless, and we began volunteering there on Sunday nights.

So many people ask me what they can do to be pro-life, or how they can get involved.

The first thing we may think of is standing up for the pre-born—and that is so important—but there are also many other things we can do.

Look around at school, work, or wherever you spend a lot of time, and ask yourself what you can do to love your neighbor. Is there an abortion mill in your town where you can pray? Are there homeless shelters near you where you can volunteer?

Wherever you live, people need to be loved, people need Christ, and people just need a friend.

How can you be more pro-life in your everyday life?

4 - Loving, Compassionate Pro-life vs. Angry Anti-abortion

This whole idea should seem like a no-brainer for Christians. It is so clear from scripture that we must love our enemies and have compassion on others. While we must take a stand against evil and share the truth, it has to be done in love.

Unfortunately, many times that is not the case when we are talking about ministry for issues like pro-life, homosexuality, and other hot-button topics.

I have seen so much anger, self-righteous attitudes, and out-right hatred in these areas.

Over the years, I have had an abundance of experiences where I saw angry anti-abortion behavior chosen over loving, compassionate pro-life behavior. I have gone to abortion mills to pray and reach out to the women only to find them being screamed at, ridiculed, insulted, and mocked by anti-abortion activists.

At a pro-life conference, I listened to a keynote speaker tell the audience we need to torture the feminists and pro-abortion-ists. Never once at this conference did I hear anything about loving them or sharing the truth about our only hope, Jesus Christ.

In a recent brochure I read about an anti-abortion event. I read it was our duty to make life a living hell for "the other side." Since when is it our job to convict people? The last time I checked that was the job of the Holy Spirit.

We, as Christians, are called to spread the gospel of Christ and to be a voice for innocent children—who are being killed an average of 4,000 times per day from surgical abortion.

"And He said to them, 'Go ye into all the world, and preach the gospel to every creature'" (Mark 16:15, KJV).

While we must be a voice for children, that voice must be a voice of love. While we may want those who are taking part in the killing of children to be convicted of their sin, we must share the truth with them in love. We must remember our place in the food chain—it's Jesus' place to convict, not ours.

"Love is patient, love is kind. It does not envy, it does not boast, it is not proud. It is not rude, it is not self-seeking, it is not easily angered, it keeps no records of wrongs. Love does not delight in evil but rejoices in the truth." (1 Corinthians 13:4-6, NIV, although I recommend that you read the whole chapter).

Stand True team member sharing stages of life in the womb at the booth at Lifest, Wisconsin, Summer 2007

Before I found the hope of Christ and His salvation, I was an evil, sinful person who lived a life of total debauchery. I was often preached at and told how evil I was and how I was going to burn in hell. I was ridiculed and looked down upon by so many religious zealots that only told me of my sin and never shared the hope and grace of Christ. I grew to hate Christians and wanted nothing to with their message.

In 1987, that all changed when I overdosed on LSD, Meth, and many other drugs and ended up in a hospital close to death. A doctor in that hospital took me outside and shared with me the love of Christ and His grace and mercy.

He told me there was hope for me, and even though I lived this life in total disregard of anything other than my own selfish pleasure, Christ would wipe all of that clean and give me a new life. One week later, God lifted me out of that horrible pit of sin and debauchery where I was living and set my feet upon the rock, Jesus Christ. He gave me a new life, and forgave me of all my sins.

"I waited patiently for the LORD; And He inclined unto me, And heard my cry. He brought me up out of an horrible pit, out of the miry clay, and set my feet upon a rock, and established my goings. He hath put a new song in my mouth, even praise unto our God: many will see it, and fear, and shall trust in the LORD" (Psalm 40:1-3, KJV).

Stand True is committed to spreading the Gospel of Christ and restoring personhood to every single person from fertilization to natural death.

We are committed to seeing an end to the killing of innocent boys and girls every day.

We want the abortion mills to be closed and the evil practice of abortion to be stopped.

We are committed to achieving these goals in love.

And we will go to the abortion mills to be a voice for those who are dying horrible deaths there. But we will treat the abortion mill like a mission field rather than a protest zone.

Not only do we want to see babies lives saved, we want to see hearts changed and souls saved.

5 - In Focus

At first glance the old Turner Schoolhouse in Rockford, Illinois looked pretty normal.

Looking at it made me think of little kids running down the hall or playing in the yard. I could imagine girls skipping rope and boys playing dodge ball.

At first glance it brought pleasant thoughts of innocent youth.

Bryan and tour team reading Scripture outside the abortion mill in Rockford, Illinois, Summer 2005

I got out of the car and walked over to the sidewalk, and the images I'd imagined quickly disappeared. Up in one of the windows was a chicken hanging from a noose. In another window was a casket with a nun in it. All over the building were speakers and closed circuit cameras pointing out at the sidewalks. In the front corner of the lawn was a big sign with two shotguns on it that read Fort Turner Abortion Clinic.

It was hard to believe this former schoolhouse, which once echoed with little voices playing and learning, was now being used to murder children. The joy I'd had as I envisioned images and voices now turned to horror as I held back the tears. I thought about the news and how we are fed up with violence in schools, yet this school was used solely for violence.

I wondered, where are all the preachers and religious leaders who cry out on the news for the children killed in schools? Why aren't they crying out for the little babies being murdered openly in this old school?

On the sidewalk, a handful of Christians gather to pray and offer counseling to women who go into the clinic. Inside, a man who lives in the building yells obscenities through the loud speakers and blasts obnoxious music trying to distract them.

In spite of his efforts, those praying out front faithfully show up every time the abortion mill opens. Although I was only visiting Rockford that day, the faithful residents were happy to have someone else join their efforts.

This particular abortion mill happens to be in Rockford, but there are different buildings all over the country where this violence takes place every day.

Chances are, you pass one by as you are going to work or school or are out running errands.

At first glance you may not even realize what is going on.

I want to encourage you to take a closer look at what is going on in your community. Look in the phone book, and find out if there is an abortion mill in your neighborhood. Next time you drive by it, stop and look at the building for what it is—a place where babies are being *murdered*, people who have no voice to cry out.

Can you be their voice? Can you cry out for them? Or will you just drive by and ignore the silent screams of these innocent children as they are being led away to slaughter?

"Rescue those being led away to death, hold back those staggering toward slaughter" (Proverbs 24:11, NIV).

6 - They, too, are America

Langston Hughes wrote a poem entitled *I, Too* in which he dreamed of a day when African-Americans would not be shunned. *I, Too* speaks volumes about personhood and the struggle to attain equality.

Corrie ten Boom wrote a book entitled *The Hiding Place* in which she talked about her days in a concentration camp. She was not Jewish; she was imprisoned and tortured for hiding Jews in her home because she believed they were equal human persons.

Rosa Parks sat down on a bus and refused to get up from a seat she was told she had no right to sit in. She decided that she was no longer going to be told that she was less human than anyone else.

Anne Frank wrote in her diary, "I don't think of all the misery, but of the beauty that still remains." This came from a young woman living in a hidden apartment for two years because she was declared a non-human person.

Martin Luther King, Jr. cried out, "I have a dream." He believed in a world where people were not looked at as black or white, but as people. He believed we could live as equal human persons and destroy the prejudices that plagued humankind.

What do all these people have in common?

Some may say oppression. Oppression is certainly a word that can be used to describe all of their lives. Can you imagine yourself as young girl like Anne Frank living in a small hidden apartment for two years, never allowed to leave for fear of certain death?

Some may say determination. Langston Hughes was determined to see a day when our African-American brothers would not be seen as less than any other American.

Some may say courage. I can't imagine the courage it took for Corrie ten Boom to risk her own life and freedom for total strangers. She endured years of torture and even found a way to thank God for her bunk being infested with fleas— knowing it saved her from abuse.

Some may say resolve. Oh, to see the resolve in the face of Rosa Parks on the bus that day! To see her claim her spot as an equal human person and her refusal to be dehumanized any longer.

Some may say passion. Passion is one of the best words you can use to describe Dr. Martin Luther King, Jr. When you hear one of his speeches, you can't help but be moved.

While all of these words truly describe what these great humans had in common, one other thing that makes them stand out from others who have been dehumanized: their voice. They each had a voice and used that voice to cry out for their lives, their freedom, and their humanity.

A voice is something that thousands of innocent people every day in America will never have.

Can you imagine if a child in the womb could write a poem about how one day he, too, would be called an American? Can you imagine if babies who were not going to be killed by abortion could hide others who were scheduled for death? Can you imagine if the abortionist tried to kill a young girl, and the child was able to sit down in the womb with resolve and say, "I will not be killed"? Can you imagine the speech a young child would give proclaiming the day all innocent pre-born children will be counted as human?

While we know these things are impossible for the children in the womb to accomplish, they are not impossible for us. We do have a voice; we now need to find the courage, determination, resolve, and passion to fight against the oppression of innocent children.

Some may say, "How dare you compare abortion with the holocaust or oppression of African-Americans!"

I say how dare we not.

How dare we look back at some of the most brutal, dehumanizing acts in history and not also include the killing of innocent babies?

We have ushered in a new era in America in 2009. With the election of Barack Obama to the presidency, we are seeing something many people believed would not happen in their lifetime. We are witnessing something we should all be proud of regardless of our political views. America has taken one more step towards equality and wiping out racial prejudices.

So many people do not believe they will see the killing of innocent children stop in their lifetime, either. So many people have accepted the abortion holocaust as status quo. I refuse to accept or believe that we cannot defeat this evil.

It is time to adopt the words that describe these great humans I wrote about.

It is time to believe that we will usher in an era where pre-born children are considered full human persons.

It is time to use our voices to proclaim life and freedom for the thousands of our brothers and sisters who die needlessly every day.

Stand True member talking with a pregnant mother at the booth, Soulfest, New Hampshire, Summer 2006

It is time to say, "They, too, America."

7 - Abortion Terminology and Hate Speech

Bryan speaking at Cornerstone Festival, Illinois, Summer 2007

I find it fascinating how many people think that by simply saying, "Abortion is the killing of a human person," I am somehow practicing hate speech. It seems like even those who are opposed to the killing of innocent human persons are reluctant to call it just that: *killing*.

Some have even told me not to use the word abortion because it might offend someone who has had one if they have to think about what they have done. The crazy part about this is that these statements often come from those who call themselves Christian and pro-life. Although I would never condemn a woman for past mistakes—remembering that that isn't my purpose in life—I will call it like I see it. Abortion = murder.

I recently got an email from a Christian who was furious at me for using the term "abortionist." He was appalled that I would refer to someone who performs abortions as an abortionist because that is saying he wants to commit abortions. Are you as confused by this as I was when I read his e-mail? I actually had to read it a couple of times through just to make sure I was not misreading it.

I explained to him that "abortionist" was simply a technical term such as therapist, anesthesiologist, or scientist. He claimed that no one wants to perform abortions, and using a term like that was hateful. I actually think that using the term is *too* kind; abortionists don't deserve professional titles.

In almost any genre, field, clique, movement, or belief system, you will find terminology that is unique and not often known outside of that group.

You will find that, inside the pro-life movement, people often refuse to call the building in which abortions are performed "clinics;" they often refer to them as "abortion mills." A clinic is a place where people go for healing, not to have someone else killed. The term "abortion mill" comes from the fact that most of these places cycle through large groups of mothers in short periods of time, much like any other mill would do, and kill the largest quantity of babies in the shortest periods of time. Therefore, we call it a mill.

Another term often used is "pro-abortion" instead of the inaccurate term coined by the abortion industry, "pro-choice."

The simple answer to this is that if someone is "pro-" the right to abortion then they are pro-abortion: this is just basic logic here.

Most pro-lifers will also refuse to say, "terminate a pregnancy." We call it what it really is: child-killing. I refuse to refer to a child in the womb as a "pregnancy."

Why do we feel the need to sanitize abortion and not call it what it really is—the killing of a human person? Why do we have to change everything not to hurt people's feelings by using correct and proper terms?

I understand that there have been some harsh aspects of the pro-life movement. And I think those people have no business being involved in the movement.

I believe we need to love those who have been hurt by abortion and be compassionate in our work. I don't think we need to scream and yell at people, but rather love them and offer them hope.

In the same manner I refuse to dishonor the more than fifty million full human persons who have been killed by abortion by referring to them as "terminated pregnancies," I will never afford the term "doctor" to a person who uses their God-given talents to rip babies limb from limb and leave many mothers hurting for the rest of their lives.

Why is it we only want to tiptoe around the atrocities of abortion and not other heinous crimes?

Imagine if someone started calling rapists "involuntary sex partners" just to soften the term so there is not as much stigma in the name? What if we called murder "post-pregnancy termination" so it would not make the person who committed the murder feel bad for what they had done? Maybe we could call people who believe it is okay to molest children "pro-choice" because they should have the choice to do what they believe?

I hope you find these examples ludicrous: I do.

What I find more ludicrous is when I am told I am using hate speech for call the killing of an innocent human person "homicide."

I find it unthinkable to reduce the lives of precious babies to be defined simply as "choices."

That, to me, is the real hate speech.

8 - Will You Light Up the Darkness, or Take Refuge in Apathy?

If you found out that your local bank was giving away free money to anyone who walked in and said the words, "Free money," would you take advantage of that? After you tried it and it worked, wouldn't you tell all your family and friends about it?

Have you ever wondered what you would do if you had been alive during the peak of the Civil Rights Movement? Would you have marched with Martin Luther King Jr.? Would you have been willing to face persecution to stand up for the rights of those who were treated as less than human?

If you were in church on Sunday morning and the speaker got up and said a man with a knife was about to go into the nursery and kill all the two-year-old children, would you try and stop him? Would you run as fast as you could to the nursery and do whatever you could to protect those innocent little children?

Stand True prayer walk through New York City, Summer 2006

I would assume that most people reading these questions would answer "Yes" to all three.

Let me rephrase them a bit and see what your answer is.

I would love to tell my family and friends about the opportunity to get even one thousand dollars for free. I know many people who would be helped greatly by a thousand dollars being handed to them. But, I can just imagine how quickly this would spread and lines would be formed for miles outside of a bank.

What if I knew of something even better than a thousand dollars that was being handed out freely?

The Bible tells us in Romans 6:23 (NIV), "For the wages of sin is death, but the gift of God is eternal life in Christ Jesus our Lord."

How much more valuable is eternal life with Christ than a thousand dollars?

How about our question about living in the days of the Civil Rights Movement? I would bet most people I know would answer, "Yes," to getting involved. They would be willing to march and face whatever persecution came their way for taking a stand. Most people would say it would be an honor to be persecuted for standing up for those who have had their personhood stripped away.

We really don't have to imagine what it would be like to live in a time when our fellow human person was being treated as less than human. It is happening today. Every day in this country thousands of our brothers and sisters have their civil rights violated and are killed unjustly. We live in a time when an entire group of people is dehumanized; their personhood has been stripped away.

Only this time, it is not because of the color of their skin, but because of their age.

The third question is really a no-brainer. Of course we would run to the nursery if we knew someone was going to go in and kill every two-year-old in the Sunday school classroom.

I honestly do not know a single person who would not do whatever it took to save the lives of those children.

So let's change the location of the incident and the age of the children.

Now it is a so-called "medical clinic" and the age of the children to be killed is twelve weeks. The same man is going to walk into the building with a knife or a scalpel and will actually be paid *by the parents* of that child to end that young life.

Will we try and intervene on behalf of the child?

Ask yourself the following questions about the children in both scenarios:

- Don't both have a heartbeat?
- Don't both have fingers and toes?
- Don't both have fingerprints and toeprints?

- Don't both have brainwaves and feel pain?
- Don't both have blood circulating throughout their bodies?
- Don't both have a soul?
- Weren't both created by God?
- Don't both live with their mother and father? Albeit one lives in his room while the other lives in his mother's womb.

While both are full human persons, one's *life* is protected by law, and the other's *death* is protected by law.

It is easy to answer a "what if" question. When it is a hypothetical situation, it is simple to give the simple answer. When the situation is facing us head on, sometimes it is not so simple.

How many of our friends or family members do we know who are not Christians? Are we excited to share with them the amazing free gift of eternal life with Christ?

Most people would like to think they would be willing to face persecution in order to have the opportunity to have marched with Martin Luther King, Jr. But would we be willing to face that same persecution to stand up for the thousands of babies who have their personhood stripped away every day?

I recently watched the movie *I am Legend,* and one of the lines in the movie was very powerful. Toward the end of the movie Will Smith's character says, "Light up the darkness."

Darkness is not the opposite of light, *but the absence thereof.*

So my question to you is simple: will you light up the darkness? Will you share the hope you have in Christ with a hopeless world? Will you take a stand for truth and life, even when you may be persecuted for your actions? Will you do something to save the lives of innocent children who are being killed by the thousands every day?

Will you light up the darkness, or take refuge in apathy?

9 - Being a Light When You Least Expect It

In 2009, I was honored when I was invited to Australia to help with the launching of Youth for Life Australia. I had met Prue Neberding, the president of Youth for Life Australia in Ireland while speaking at the Youth Defence (Irish spelling) pro-life activists conference in the spring of 2006. Prue and I have had the pleasure of working together for several years now, and I was ecstatic when she asked me to come down to Australia.

One of events in Australia was a pro-life fundraising dinner for Youth for Life, the organization that brought us to Australia. We had just finished an all day pro-life training conference where we talked with the Australians about the different aspects of the pro-life movement in America. We shared about some of the events, educational resources, and programs we have developed and gave ideas on how to adapt and use them in Australia. It was a nice way to end the day by sharing a great meal with all of our new Aussie friends.

On my first day there, Marcel White, the director of Right to Life Australia gave me a tour of Melbourne, which included several abortion mills. We took pictures and discussed some of the pro-life strategies for ministry at these abortion mills. The logical next step in the conversation was football. Marcel loved explaining how their Aussie-rules football was so much bet-ter than American gridiron football. He and I threw jabs about which sport was better and who was tougher. Marcel then invited me to a game between his favorite team, the Hawthorne Hawks, and the team I chose to support, the Geelong Cats. Being involved in the

Bryan hanging out backstage before a Pillar show with the band and friends, Kingdom Bound Festival, New York, Summer 2006

pro-life movement makes for strange ways in which people get to know each other.

During the dinner I gave a talk, and was followed by Marcel. So, as Marcel stood up to give his talk that night, I was very happy because he was wearing a Cats scarf. (He had lost a friendly wager on the game the night before.) When he brought up the game in his talk, I was waiting for him to rail against American football again, but that is not what he wanted to talk about. He mentioned how he watched me talking to people in the stadium about abortion.

I obviously stood out with my loud, American accent, and everywhere I went in Australia, people asked me if I was American or Canadian. The next question I always got was, "What are you doing in Australia?"

This is what caught Marcel's attention: I immediately would tell people I was there to speak about pro-life. They would always ask what I meant by that. And I would explain that I believed abortion was the killing of an innocent human person, and we are trying to bring an end to it.

When Marcel brought this up, I thought about my travels over the last month throughout Europe and Australia. I began to think about the plane rides and long conversations with people around me on the plane. On one of my flights the gentlemen next to me immediately said, "We will drop this conversation," when I told him I was a pro-life speaker. But within minutes we actually had a good conversation about God and about pro-life.

I actually love flights because of conversations I get to have with people about God, being pro-life, and so many other subjects. I thought about the girl I sat next to on my flight to Australia who watched Bill Maher's *Religulous* with me on my computer. I was able to talk to her and some of the people around me about Christ and what true Christianity is about.

We are part of couchsurfing.org. CouchSurfing is a worldwide network for making connections between travelers and the communities they visit. I thought about the couch-surfing hosts we had in Poland who asked me why we were in Europe. When they filled out a reference on my CouchSurfing.com profile, they mentioned my respect for life and how they admired that.

I realized when I take these trips to talk at events around the world, I end up talking to so many more people than ever come to the events. I end up in situations all the time where I have a chance to share Christ and the message of life.

In fact, just the other night as I talked to the RotoRooter man who was fixing our plumbing, he shared with me how his ex-girlfriend had had an abortion behind his back years ago, and how much it had hurt him.

Marcel brought up the story about talking to people at the football game to encourage people always to be prepared to be a light in the darkness. He wanted to challenge us always to look for situations where we can share our message and to be willing to do so at any time.

Abortion is not a pleasant topic of conversation and can really make a conversation heavier than expected. I realize most people don't want to talk about abortion; it is kind of a sickening topic. I have lost many friends over the years because they just get tired of my turning every topic back to abortion. They complain that I just talk about it too much.

I have no apologies for this, and as long as babies are dying each day, I will not stop talking about it. I really don't care if I lose every friend I have. I will not be silent as a sizeable portion of a generation is being systematically slaughtered.

I wonder if Dr. Martin Luther King, Jr. ever chilled out and stopped talking about civil rights because his friends were sick of hearing about it. I wonder if William Wilberforce ever cared about how many friends he lost because of his relentless fight to end the slave trade. I know I can never come close to matching the greatness of these men, but I can look to them as inspiration.

People tell me this issue is too complicated, and there is no point in doing what I do. I am told it will always exist so I might as well accept it. So many people think abortion is just too controversial, and they don't want to offend people or make waves.

The only thing controversial about abortion, in my opinion, is that it still exists.

I don't find it complicated at all. Abortion is the killing of an innocent human person and therefore must be stopped. Just because something will still exist does not make it right. Many heinous crimes exist that we don't decriminalize simply because they still occur!

People can give me every reason in the world why I need to stop being so obsessed with life, and it will never slow me down, nor will it stop me.

Marcel, my Australian friend, saw a trait in me that some people don't like and think is negative. Marcel found inspiration in that part of my life, and I thank God for that.

I know that he…

(OK, I am seriously in tears right now, as I am picking up where I stopped in mid-sentence in the last paragraph. I had to stop because the sewage treatment company showed up to give us an estimate on our basement, which flooded with sewage. I mentioned earlier about the RotoRooter man, how he shared with me his pain, and how I was able to talk with him. The sewage treatment man asked what I do, as he noticed my tattoos. I told him I ran a pro-life organization, and he shared with me how his brother just told him he was thinking of having his girlfriend get an abortion. He said he had no idea how to talk to him about this. I was able to give him some literature and a fetal model to share with his brother and his brother's girlfriend, and go over some talking points.)

I love how God can use something as disgusting as a sewage back-up to work for His glory. It makes me want to leave the office and just walk around places so people will ask me what I do. I honestly can't wait for my next flight so I can see what God will do next.

If you have a cool story about how God used you in the most unusual way, I would love to read about it.

Oh yeah, and going back to finish that sentence… I know

that he understands why I am willing to dedicate my life to being a voice for the voiceless, and he is willing to do the same.

10 – The Ten Commandments and Exceptions in Abortion Laws

Imagine that, when God gave Moses the Ten Commandments, Moses had wondered whether people would accept them as they were. Being a good leader, Moses might have decided they were just too harsh, and he should introduce them incrementally—or maybe just add exceptions so the people would accept them quicker.

What if they read:

1. Thou shall not bear false witness on thy neighbor (except when you are in an embarrassing situation and need a quick way out of it).
2. Thou shall not steal (except when you think the price is too high).
3. Thou shall not commit adultery (except when your spouse is in a coma).
4. Thou shall not commit murder (except when a situation arises in which your life may be inconvenienced due to the presence of children).

Imagine then, when some people complain that these are too strict, the adultery commandment would also provide an exception for when your spouse is out of town, or if you find out she has upset you in some way.

I hope you find this to be ludicrous.

When you teach the Ten Commandments to your children, do you add exceptions to them? Do you tell them that they are just suggestions?

God's law is not something to be played with to fit our needs and ideas. The Ten Commandments have been set by God for a reason, and we do not have the right to judge what we will or will not obey, depending on our circumstances. Certain things in life are just plain wrong.

Bryan speaking in front of the U.S. Capitol building at a crossroads event, Washington DC, Summer 2006

"Thou shall not commit murder" cannot be any clearer. Murder is something we all know is wrong, and whether we try to justify it or not, it does not change God's absolute truth. If you ask any child if it is okay to kill a baby, he or she will tell you, "NO!"

Now, why is it politicians—who are supposed to be our well-educated, strong-principled leaders—can't see this? Why is it they try to distort the truth? Why is it, when it comes to laws that outlaw the murder of innocent children in the womb, they suddenly forget what it means to follow the commandment, "Thou shall not kill"?

I believe it is because they are concerned with re-election and what people may say about them, not with doing what is right, and what they were voted into office to do, which is to represent the people. They need to represent all people, including those who are still in the womb. Suddenly they are lifting themselves above God's law and deciding the commandant about murder is too harsh, and we should have exceptions to it so we can please the voters.

I am not just talking about politicians who are not Christians. I am talking about men and women who profess Christ and then deny God's truth with their actions. They have fallen into the lie that they must be pragmatic about their approaches to passing laws; they must base their actions on the possible outcomes instead of the truth they know in their hearts.

By doing this, whose will are they bowing to—man or God? Who are they trying to please? I would ask them to think beyond whom they will answer to on this earth—and remember whom they will answer to when they die.

When I talk to people, I am often told I could never be a politician. I do not have the ability to compromise. I say praise God for that. I may not be a politician, but I am a voter.

I don't look at elections on the basis of who has the best chance of winning. I look for someone I believe in, and that is whom I will vote for, whether they have a chance of winning or not. I know that some people will tell me that my vote is no good then—it is wasted. I ask them to show me precisely how, by voting for someone who puts God's truth aside, I am winning. What am I winning? What is anybody winning?

I acknowledge we are stuck with a two-party system. But I refuse to believe we cannot change that. The more people who vote for what is right instead of who they think can win, the better the chance that we can actually get things done.

We cannot continue to settle for the scraps the Democrats and Republicans throw us, or things will never change.

I, for one, refuse to believe that standing on principle and rejecting compromise will get me nowhere. Christ stood on principle and truth and never compromised. He paid the ultimate price and was crucified on the cross so we may be set free. It is His courage and faithfulness to us that motivate me to stand on His truth. I know, without a shadow of a doubt, that the truth will set us free.

I will continue to pray that our nation's leaders will turn to the truth and be set free from the bondage of compromise.

11 – Love Your Neighbor as Yourself

"And thou shalt love the Lord thy God with all thy heart, and with all thy soul, and with all thy mind, and with all thy strength: this is the first commandment. And the second is like, namely this, Thou shalt love thy neighbor as thyself. There is none other commandment greater than these." (Mark 12:30-31, KJV)

Is your neighbor just the person who lives next door to you or the person who lives across the street?

In Luke 10, a lawyer asked Jesus, "Who is my neighbor?"

Jesus answered with the parable of the Good Samaritan. Jesus explained that a Levite and a priest traveling down a road both saw a man in need in a ditch and just passed him up, not offering any help. Then a Samaritan saw him and helped him. The Samaritan loved his neighbor as himself.

Who is our neighbor? I would say anyone in our path who is in need is our neighbor. If we see a homeless man and give him food, we are showing love to our neighbor. And even if this man does not live next door to us, he is our neighbor.

So let's ask ourselves how we would want someone to love us if we were in danger. If our lives were in danger and our neighbor knew about it, would we not want them to help us? Would we expect someone to speak up for us if we were sentenced to death unjustly? That would be expecting others to live by this command to love their neighbor as themselves.

I have heard that verse thousands of times in my life, taught it in churches, at youth groups, and many other places. It seems to be a favorite verse to teach us how we should treat others, and I agree it is a great teaching verse.

I would say, however, that for the most part the "capital-C Church" has ignored this verse when it comes to children in the womb unjustly sentenced to death by abortion. It is easy to get people to volunteer for things like feeding the homeless or donating to causes. But when I talk about standing up for our neighbor in the womb, the comment I get so often is, "I'm not called to it."

I wonder, did the Good Samaritan stop and ask God if he was "called to a ditch ministry"? Does this verse say love your neighbor if you are called to that particular need?

Is there an abortion mill close to you? Do you pass one on your way to work every day? Do you ever stop to think what is really going on in that building? Does it register with you that inside that building your neighbor is about to be butchered brutally?

For the most part, I would bet that none of us want to think about this because it makes us uncomfortable. We would never want to see the results of what goes on in these buildings because it is too disturbing.

Do you find yourself passing by thinking, "What a shame"?

What if it was you in that building, and some man or woman was about to tear you limb from limb? What if your neighbors were passing by and knew what was going on, yet just passed on by because they were too busy, or did not want to think about what was going to happen to you?

Yes, that seems ridiculous to think about.

What if it was a daycare center, and we saw a man walking in with a butcher knife? What if you could actually see him walking towards the kids on the playground? I would bet money that you would stop and do whatever you could to prevent him from reaching those children.

Unfortunately, the children entering into the abortion mill are not seen, and we don't get that emotional bond we would if we saw them playing on a playground. Abortion has become so political that we are clouded as to what is really going on in that building. If we truly saw it for what it actually is, I do not believe that it would still be legal thirty years after Roe v. Wade.

So I ask you, "Who is your neighbor?" Are you willing to love your neighbor as yourself? Are you willing to live by what Christ taught us in the parable?

We can love our neighbor and be a voice for those who do not have one in so many ways.

1. Adopt an abortion mill for which to pray. Go to StandTrue.com, click on the link for "Prayer for

Abortion Provider Project," and follow the steps.

2. Volunteer at a local crisis pregnancy center.
3. Sidewalk counsel and pray at a local abortion mill.
4. Have a pro-life rally in your area to get people involved. (We would love to help you with this, and can provide a speaker for you. E-mail us at info@standtrue.com.)
5. Organize a drive to collect baby items at your church for your local crisis pregnancy center.
6. Start a Stand True chapter in your area, and spread the pro-life message.
7. Distribute pro-life literature, and educate your friends.
8. Get educated on all pro-life issues so you can take a stand, and prepare solid arguments for debate.
9. Spread the message on the Internet through Twitter, Facebook, MySpace, and e-mail forwards. You can use anything from the Stand True website or e-mails to get the message out.
10. Donate to Stand True. Stand True is starting with limited funds and needs to raise money to continue our work. A donation of any size will help.

It does not matter which of these you choose to do, or if you choose to stand up in another way, as long as you stand up.

Stand True team members praying outside
abortion mill, Philadelphia, Summer 2007

12 - Can We Stand on a Broken Foundation?

For more than thirty-six years, our generation has suffered losses unequaled in history. Surgical abortion has eliminated more than fifty million of our brothers and sisters with countless others eliminated by chemical abortion, such as birth control and the "morning after" pill.

Stand True team members reading scripture outside abortion mill, Richmond, Virginia, Spring 2006

Every year, we hear about groups of kids being killed in schools, churches, and various other places. We see the pictures on the news and cry along with the parents of these children. We see our nation's "Christian" leaders speaking out and calling for an end to this violence. We see our President and other politicians get angry, promising to pass stricter laws to protect our nation's children. We see the police spending countless hours investigating these crimes. We see citizens outraged that this is happening in America. We cannot escape these scenes. They are broadcast on every radio and television station in the country. America cries loud for the blood of her children—or does she?

In many states laws are in place that make it a homicide to kill a baby in the womb while attacking a pregnant woman, yet in the same state, the same pregnant woman can pay someone to have her child killed by a doctor.

If we pass laws to protect some children in the womb, why are our politicians not passing laws to protect all children in the womb? The answer is simple: they do not see them as real children.

Should we blame this on the pro-abortion forces? Partly. There is, however, another reason.

We must blame ourselves—the pro-life movement—and our contradiction in terms.

We maintain that life begins at conception (fertilization), but we then allow drugs that kill babies days after conception. We say that all human life is of equal value and should be protected, and then concede that those conceived in rape or incest are exceptions to this rule.

"But everyone who hears these words of mine and does not put them into practice is like a foolish man who built his house on sand," says Matthew 7:26 (NIV).

We have destroyed our own pro-life foundation with our hypocrisy. We have given in to the rhetoric and lost sight of our goals. We have devalued the child in the womb to being merely an issue or an arguing point. We have, by our own efforts, stripped away the most important aspect of these other children—their personhood.

Every living person should have the same inalienable rights. The manner in which they were conceived, the condition of their health, or the condition of the mother's health should never determine the personhood of anyone. The moment we place value on one life over another, we have compromised the personhood of all. How can we pass laws that would protect some and allow the deaths of others? What is the defining point that makes one life valuable and the other expendable?

The moment we concede to this flawed logic, we destroy the foundation of our position that life exists from the moment of conception until its natural conclusion. The personhood of that life is no longer an absolute truth; it has become relative. At that point we have become guilty of devaluing human life.

Truth can never change. It is without compromise, and we must stand on the truth in all of our work. We must never stray from the truth to seek interim results, or for any other reason. God is our ultimate authority, and we must simply do the work that He has put in front of us. We must stand completely on His truth and His power in this work, for the victory is not ours. It is God's.

If we continue on the path of compromise, then we are just as guilty as those who look away and ignore the cries of the innocent. We must rebuild our foundation on solid truth. We must declare the truth and insist on the value of personhood without exception for every single life conceived. If we waver from this truth, we are destined to fail.

If we stand solid and do not compromise God's truth, we will succeed.

section two

pro-life responses to events

Amber's Dream

Little Amber in pigtails,
Skipping rope in the sun,
Playing in the meadows,
Running through the fields.
Lemonade stand on the corner,
Dollies all dressed up,
Baby doll in her arms,
Amber's **dreaming** of future plans.

Little Amber **growing** up,
Starting Jr. High School,
Giggling with her friends,
Talking on the phone.
Passing notes in English class,
Starting to notice boys,
Babysitting on weekends,
Amber's **dreaming** of future plans.

Little Amber in her dress,
Prom is coming soon.
She looked so beautiful
As she stood **daydreaming**.
High school almost over,
Maybe someday marriage,
Amber's **dreaming** of future plans.

Little Amber all in tears,
She'd made a grave mistake.
She **listened** to their lies,
And taken their advice.
Her **heart ripped** in pieces,
Childhood dreams destroyed.
They **killed** her baby today,
Amber's dream is in a garbage can.

13 – History:
Can You Hear the Silence?

One hundred and fifty years ago, nine men sat upon a bench that was designed to bring equal justice under law to all Americans and disgraced their office. They lifted themselves above God Almighty and declared black people were not fully human. This atrocity is something we teach in our schools as one of the darkest moments in American history.

Thirty-seven years ago, nine men sat upon a bench that was designed to bring equal justice under law to all Americans and disgraced their office. They lifted themselves above God Almighty and declared that pre-born babies were not fully human. This atrocity is something we teach in our schools as one of the greatest moments in American history.

These two devastating acts ushered in two very dark and tragic chapters of American history. These decisions have been responsible for the death of millions of Americans and have brought shame on our nation. One of these chapters was brought to a close long ago, while the other is still open and still stains our nation's streets with the blood of innocents.

Bryan outside the old courthouse where the Dred Scott trial took place, St. Louis, Missouri, Summer 2006

So here we are, more than thirty-seven years later, and still almost 4,000 babies are killed every day in our country. That is one-and-a-half million children taken from the safety of their mothers' wombs every year in the name of "choice."

It is hard to imagine these numbers sometimes. They just seem so unreal.

Let's look at an event in our recent history that has caused the whole world to react. The tsunamis in southern Asia claimed over 140,000 lives in one day. The devastation there brought an outpouring of humanitarian relief and aid unlike anything this world has probably ever seen.

140,000 lives lost. That is equal to about thirty-five days of abortion. That would be about eleven tsunamis hitting America with equal loss of life every year. We would have had to have over 350 tsunamis hit our shores since January 22, 1973, all with equal loss of life, to match how many children have been killed by surgical abortion alone.

Where is the outpouring of humanitarian aid for this loss of life? Where are all the news stories about people who are trying to figure out ways to avoid this holocaust? Where are God's people thirty-four years later? What are we waiting for?

If you think that voting for a conservative candidate will solve the problem, think again.

If you think that appointing a couple of Supreme Court justices will overturn Roe v. Wade, just look back to Ronald Reagan.

We have not done enough, and political victories mean nothing until hearts have changed.

As the people in Southern Asia fled from the tsunami and were rescued, as they clung to floating objects and trees, they were able to cry out for help. The children who will die today from abortion are not able to cry out. They need a voice.

Listen carefully. Can you hear it? Can you hear the deafening silence of the third of this generation about to die? Will you be a voice for the voiceless? Will you break the silence?

14 - The News
(Can We Really Call it That?)

I remember, as a kid, that I used to hate to watch the news because it was full of what I considered "boring stuff." They were always talking about what was going on in the world, and I hated it.

As an adult, I grew to like the news. I wanted to be informed of what was going on in the world and know about important events. Unfortunately, the news stations don't seem to care about what's important anymore.

Bryan speaking on main stage, Purple Door Festival, Pennsylvania, Summer 2008

I have been trying to watch the news while walking on the treadmill at the gym this week, and all I see and hear about is the fight for Anna Nicole Smith's body and how much Britney Spears' hair should sell for on E-bay. What is wrong with our nation that allows these two things to become the top stories of the week? I knew the news was turning into a joke, but this is beyond what I could have ever imagined. I shaved my head this week. Why is CNN not following me around?

Here's some real news you may not have heard about this week, because it's actually important. Several states have passed, or are trying to pass, laws that make it mandatory for girls as young as nine to be vaccinated for HPV (Human Papillomavirus), an STD.

This goes right along with what Planned Parenthood and the abortion industry are trying to teach our youth: that they are just animals, with no self-control, who will have sex no matter what. They don't believe it is possible for young people to remain pure.

What kind of message are we sending the young women of this nation? Many high schools put wrecked cars in front of their schools to show kids what happens when you drink and drive. Maybe the same should be done with the stories of popular celebrities whose lives are train wrecks.

My oldest daughter is going to be eight-years-old in three months. The media must think I'm insane because I believe my daughters will remain pure until their wedding day, like their mother did.

It all comes back to one thing: this world needs Christ. But then, the news stations might get sued if they talked about that. (Unfortunately, Christ never went to rehab, and He rose from the dead before we got the chance to fight over His body.)

15 - 09/11/2001 and 01/22/1973: Two Days of Infamy

On September 11, 2001, we saw two horrific attacks on the World Trade Center and the Pentagon. We know almost 3,000 human persons were killed on that one day. I have mourned and prayed along with most of the world over this tragic loss of human life.

I have also listened to and read statements by world leaders, religious leaders, celebrities, and organizations about how precious human life is. I have listened as they called our nation to prayer and talked about God blessing our nation. I have even seen groups like Planned Parenthood and NOW talk about the tragic loss of human life.

I have watched as true American heroes are honored for their bravery, and rightfully so.

With all due respect and sympathy for those who were killed on 09-11—a day that is being remembered everywhere—I say that we are missing the bigger picture.

I call to your attention another "day of infamy" we all should mourn, 01-22-73—the day personhood was stripped away from the most helpless and the youngest American people, preborn children. More than 50,000,000 Americans have been the victims of cruel disregard for human life because of a decision made that day.

Bryan's son, Jaemison, with a friend of the Kemper family at the March for Life 2007, Washington DC

I do not understand how organizations like Planned Parenthood can talk about this tragic loss of human life and at the same time destroy children every day.

I do not understand how Congress can come together in one day and pass legislation that will allow us to put an end to one form of terrorism, yet ignore the plight of so many helpless children. Hundreds of entertainers pooled their talents to raise money for the victims and their families of those killed on 09-11-01, but those same "artists" have helped raise money to promote the deaths sanctioned on 01-22-73.

I, too, have the utmost respect for the firefighters and policemen and EMTs who risked their lives and worked so hard to save others' lives. I would call them true American heroes. It is great that our government has called them heroes and is honoring them. But at the same time, the government persecutes other men and women who have given most of their lives to defending human life.

Joseph Scheidler is one of my greatest heroes. He is an unsung hero who has given decades of his life to fight for the lives of precious little babies. He is being sued and called a "racketeer" for his selfless, heroic work on behalf of the babies. And there is "Doc," a very elderly man who sits outside an abortion mill in Portland, Oregon, for hours, nearly every day, witnessing to the truth and offering help to young women. Why are these true American heroes not being honored for their work?

I am in no way trying to minimize what happened on 09-11-01, but I do want to bring the attention of the world to what is still happening as a result of the events of 01-22-73. Our generation has lost over one-third of its brothers and sisters, and we cannot let this go unrecognized by so many Americans any longer. The world has had a wake-up call and has felt the impact of the loss of thousands of lives. The world needs to see the devastation that has been wrought on a generation that has lost millions.

As I mourn with our nation over 09-11-01, I also mourn over our nation's callous attitude toward the fateful decisions made on 01-22-73. I cry over the fact that the events of 09-11-01 inspire thousands to fill Yankee Stadium for a prayer service, yet, when we ask people to pray for those who will be lost to abortion, only a handful show up. I am angered by organizations that can call life "precious" one day, and the next, fight for the right to kill babies. I weep for those who shed tears and raised money for one group of people who are suffering, but empty their wallets to help destroy another group of people.

I know what I have written here may anger or upset some people, but I hope and pray that it will anger you, too, that babies are being murdered, and that our country does not shed tears for them. As for myself and all the rest here at Stand True, we will shed tears for all human persons who are killed, born and pre-born alike. The nineteen terrorists who crashed their planes into those buildings stripped away the personhood of thousands. The abortion industry has stripped away the personhood of millions. Our job is to restore personhood to every single human being no matter how small.

16 – I Did Not Watch the 2008 Beijing Olympics

I want to first make this very clear: I did not watch the Olympics as a boycott or protest. I am not telling you that you are wrong if you decided to watch the Olympics. I simply want to express why I did not sit down and enjoy the Olympics that year.

While most countries allow abortion, China takes it a step further with forced abortion. China has a one-child policy and forces women who get pregnant again to have abortions. It really amazes me that the "so called" pro-choice movement does not speak up against this. Wouldn't a forced abortion be going against the idea of choice?

China is also a staunch supporter of Sudan's government, which is committing mass genocide in Darfur. Hundreds of thousands of people have been slaughtered in Darfur, and millions have been displaced. Sudan's government is killing, raping, and torturing black Africans in Darfur, and China is helping them by supplying weapons.

With issues like forced abortion, the support of Sudan's government, the atrocities in Tibet, and so much more, it saddens me to see China looked at in such a great light during the Olympics. I know there are many other countries, including our own, who are guilty of human rights violations. I know China is not the only country to disregard human life, but they are one of the worst.

I tried to sit down, give the Olympics a chance, and watch the opening ceremonies. NBC showed a few minutes of footage about why people are angry about the Olympics being in China before they went into the celebration of the opening ceremonies. As I sat there, my heart saddened as I thought about what was more important for me. I could not help but think about all the people who were displaced in Beijing for Olympic facilities to be built. I thought about the billions of dollars spent for things like swimming pools and racetracks, as so many people in China are starving and suffering. I thought about every second child conceived in China, and the pain his or her mother went through as they were forced to kill their children simply for not being the firstborn.

As much as I like watching the Olympics, was this worth it? Is seeing someone jump higher than someone else more important than taking a stand? For me it's not worth it. I decided not to watch the Olympics. I know my not watching them will not change what is going on right now. I made this decision as a matter of principle for myself and to stand in solidarity with those who are suffering. I have decided to take some of the time I would spend watching the Olympics and use that to research more ways I can be a voice for those who have none.

Bryan and friend hanging out behind the booth, Alive Festival, Canal Fulton, Summer 2006

I want to reemphasize that I'm not telling you not to watch the Olympics or asking you to boycott them. I am simply asking you to think about some of these issues and look into how you might be a voice also.

17 - The DC Area Sniper: Where is the Justice?

Police keeping watch during prayer at abortion mill in Pittsburgh, Pennsylvania, Spring 2006

I sat down the other night to watch a made-for-TV movie about the Washington, DC sniper. I was interested in how they would show all of the events and emotions. I think I was so interested because I live in the area and experienced these tragedies firsthand.

I remember driving to the bank with my wife, telling her not to worry; everything was happening in Maryland. About a half hour later, as I was coming out of the party store, I saw her screaming. As I approached the car, she told me someone was just shot across the street from where we were. I was panicked as I sped out of the parking lot and told her to cover the kids.

A few days later, I went into DC for a conference, and I got a call on my cell phone that someone was killed at a gas station just down the road from our house.

I really began to watch the news 24/7 at that point. I think I was like everyone else in our area. I just wanted to know it was safe for my kids to go outside and play. I wanted to get gas without ducking behind my car.

As I watched the news, I got more and more upset at what I saw. I would drive down the road and see police cars at every corner. I would see helicopters everywhere. I watched as the police shut down roads and searched everyone after a shooting.

The media talked about over 1,000 federal agents and the

President being briefed at daily news conferences several times a day to keep the public informed.

I watched Chief Charles Moose crying as he talked about the sniper crossing the line when he shot a child. He was so shocked that someone could hurt a child.

I agreed with that, but I wanted to ask him a question. Why are you not putting this kind of effort into stopping the murder of innocent children in our country every day? If shooting a child in a school is crossing a line, then killing a child in the womb is just as wrong no matter what the law says. Lynching a person was legal at one time, if their skin was black. Does that change what it was? No. It was murder, and it should have been stopped, regardless of what the law said.

Hundreds of law enforcement officers are working around the clock because of thirteen shootings, meanwhile almost 4,000 innocent children are being killed every day, and law enforcement is actually protecting those killers.

Imagine if our government actually decided to protect all American citizens equally and put a stop to the bloodshed in the abortion clinics.

Imagine if all the churches that held prayer vigils and all the extra time people spent in prayer was also spent for those whose death is never shown on the news.

If we really believe that children in the womb are the same as anyone else, then we would be reacting with the same horror and urgency that we did to the sniper. Are you?

It is one year later, and the sniper is no longer killing, but one and a half million more children have been killed by abortion. Where is the justice?

18 - Terri Schiavo: Where Were You When the Battle Raged?

For nineteen years I have been involved with pro-life work in one way or another. Over those nineteen years I have talked to thousands of people about their involvement: why they got involved, how they got involved and what motivates them to continue. We have talked about what happened in 1973, and where were all the Christians when Roe v. Wade was passed. We would wonder why Christians would ignore human rights and own slaves in the time of the Dred Scott decision. We would tell stories about the few brave Christians who hid Jews during the Holocaust, and proclaim that if we were alive in those times, we would have been a voice. If we were around in those days, we would have risked all to save an innocent life. That is what we said, at least.

Several years ago a young woman in Florida who was handicapped began an agonizing and painful journey toward death. Her husband, who had once made a vow to love and honor her through good times and bad, murdered her on national television. Her husband, who had already broken his vows to her by living with another woman and fathering children with her, went to court to have his wife starved and dehydrated to death. Terri Schiavo held onto life and fought for thirteen days before finally dying on Thursday, March 31, 2005.

When I arrived in Florida one week before her death, I expected to see thousands and thousands of Christians in front of the hospice praying, singing, and crying out for Terri. I expected to see all those people who said, "I would have been there to stand up if I were around in the times of Roe v. Wade or during the Holocaust." I was sadly disappointed.

I walked up and saw maybe 150 people at most -- some of them familiar faces from the pro-life movement, some of them just wanting to be part of the media circus. I started to walk around and ask where people were from, and most of them were from out of town. It was hard to find anyone from the Tampa area there to stand up for Terri. For years I wondered where the Christians were when Roe v. Wade was passed, and now I had the answer.

I spent the first day walking around the crowd, praying with people, talking about what could be done, and simply being there in solidarity with our sister as she was dying. When I arrived the second day, I talked to Terri's sister, whom I had met in Washington, DC in January, when I volunteered my services to the family. I was asked by the family to help guard them and escort them around the hospice and through the media circus, as they were being swarmed by everyone.

I spent a lot of time just sitting with them and listening to stories about Terri and her life growing up. Her dad, Robert Schindler, told a story about when Terri ran over a cat, and how upset she was over this poor little cat. The friends shared beautiful stories and memories that I will treasure forever.

During this time, we also spent a lot of time in prayer, with many different Christian leaders and friends. Everyone would be talking about a possible option, and then someone would just stop and say, "Let's pray." There was more spontaneous prayer than I had ever seen. I would walk among the people there in support and see small groups up and down the street praying, singing hymns, and just reading the Scriptures out loud. A large group may not have been there, but those present were dedicated and focused on prayer.

I spent a lot of time walking the family through the media circus to and from the hospice, trying to give them a little privacy. I would walk Terri's dad through the crowd every night as he thanked all the supporters for being there for Terri.

I talked to many of the behind-the-scenes media people who were obviously shaken by this tragedy. I remember the look in Anderson Cooper's face after she died. He was definitely touched by her family. Several CNN producers and reporters were visibly shaken at the news of her death as they hugged me and offered condolences.

I saw people from all different walks of life and political and religious backgrounds taking a stand. Many non-Christian people were there in support of Terri, and dozens of handicapped people from a group called Not Dead Yet. I even spent time in prayer with the Rev. Jesse Jackson as he came to help the family and speak out for Terri. I never in a million years would have believed that I would sit in a room praying with Randal Terry, Jesse Jackson, and Sean Hannity.

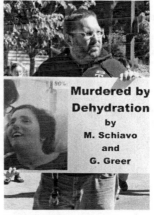

Murdered by Dehydration
by
M. Schiavo
and
G. Greer

Each night at about 11:00 PM, I would leave the hospice area, go get something to eat, try to catch up on some computer work, and grab a few hours of sleep. I talked to a lot of people at different restaurants who would ask us what was really happening there. One night Terri's brother, Bobby, came out to eat with us. When he left, the people there asked us questions and wanted to know the truth

Bryan at event with Bobby Schindler, in memory of his sister, Terri Schiavo, Philadelphia, Pennsylvania, Spring 2006

about the whole situation. They were shocked when they got the true facts about Terri.

On Wednesday night I went to the hotel and was especially saddened as we were reaching thirteen days. My friend Will and I sat in the pool at the hotel at 2:00 AM, discussing the past week and what else could have been done. I finally got to sleep at about 3:00 AM. Early the next morning, I was awakened by Will, telling me Terri had died.

We quickly packed our bags and drove over to the hospice a few blocks away. As I got into the car, it really began to hit me what had just happened, and I started to cry. I picked up my cell phone and called my wife and children. I just needed to hear their voices and tell them I loved them.

I got to the hospice and stood guard outside the room the family was in to give them some privacy. The room was tucked in behind all the major media trucks and production areas. I watched as many of the media producers and reporters were fighting back tears. I watched reporters hugging the family and giving condolences. They were truly touched by Terri's family. Many of the media I had gotten to know expressed their grief to me, some of them on-air personalities who were affected greatly.

After the family was done making their statements for the day, I made my rounds to offer my condolences and say my goodbyes. I told the family about all the Stand True supporters and family who had asked me to send their best wishes and prayers. I thanked them for their strength and resolve in the fight for Terri's life. I let them know we at Stand True will never let Terri's name die, and we will continue the fight for life and for others like Terri.

19 – Michael Vick Should Have Invested his Money in Killing Babies Instead of Dog Fighting

While the title of this commentary is meant to be sarcastic, it is sadly true. Michael could have invested his money into an abortion clinic, and he would not be in trouble, in fact he would be protected. It may be against federal law to inflict cruelty on animals but it is perfectly fine, according to the law, to dismember little baby boys and girls any time in the first nine months of their lives.

I am horrified by dog fighting, just like most people. I think it is a barbaric practice and should be illegal. I am not, however, OK with the fact that our federal government allows more protection for a dog than a human person. It is absolutely asinine that we as a society can get in an uproar about dog fighting and still allow the destruction of almost 4,000 precious children each day.

Organizations like PETA are, in their own words, "bellowing for strong action on behalf of dogs." They want the NFL to make rules about its players and their involvement in dog fighting and animal cruelty. I wonder if PETA would support the NFL if they made rules against its players being involved in paying so-called "doctors" to kill their own children.

John Rolfe, a writer for *Sports Illustrated* wrote, "Only a drooling, spiral-eyed sadist would insist that drowning, hanging, or electrocuting innocent dogs should be an non-punishable offense, let alone allowing them to rip each other to shreds for fun and profit." I wonder if he would include injecting saline into a baby while still in the womb, or suctioning their body parts off with a hose into that category.

Where are we heading as a nation if we cannot protect the most innocent and vulnerable citizens, the pre-born children, yet we can offer such protection to dogs? Since when are dogs more valuable than babies? It seems our nation has somehow granted personhood to dogs. When will we restore it to all humans? When will we say, "Enough is enough"? God have mercy on our nation, we are so blind.

Bryan's wife, Carrie, and his fifth child, Atticus, hanging out at a festival, Purple Door, Summer 2007

PETA is asking the public to demand the NFL add cruelty to animals to its personal conduct rules. I want to ask the public to ask PETA to demand the same protection for babies in the womb. I challenge PETA to show some consistency in their crusade against cruelty and work for the same protection for humans as it does for animals.

When I was speaking the other night in Dayton, Ohio, I took some time for questions and answers. After a forty-five minute talk and ten minutes of questions, a little boy raised his hand. He had sat through the whole talk, listened to everything, and offered a simple, yet poignant, question:

"Why are people so worried about saving animals, but don't care about saving babies?" the boy asked.

I ended my talk with that question.

The wisdom of a child!

20 - George Tiller: An Abortionist Was Aborted

On Sunday, May 31, 2009, abortionist George Tiller was aborted as he walked into his church. Scott Roeder decided to take the law into his own hands and abort him for what he has done to thousands of innocent little baby boys and girls.

Stand True does not believe in aborting abortionists and denounces this violent act. Answering the violence of abortion with more violence will not serve the babies or help the pro-life movement in any way. We prayed for the family of George Tiller and those in his church when he was shot. We know healing can come through Jesus and pray those involved in the abortion industry will turn to Christ.

Bryan speaking at Soulfest, a few months after Tiller was killed, where he spoke about the content of this article, New Hampshire, Summer 2009

I am sure some of you are trying to figure out why I would be so insensitive as to use the term "aborted" when referring to the murder of George Tiller. I wonder if those who think I am being insensitive are also people who would be mad when I use the term "murdered" when talking about babies who are aborted. In all reality I am being very sensitive to the abortion industry by saying he was aborted, since that is the term they like to use to describe the taking of a life.

While this may sound very sarcastic, I am truly saddened by this murder. However, I am also saddened that every day, 4,000 babies are also murdered. I am saddened that today 4,000 babies will be murdered. I am saddened that tomorrow 4,000 babies will be murdered.

I am saddened the news media will not report on the horrific fate of those 4,000 innocent babies who are just as human as, and as deserving of the same protection as George Tiller.

I am saddened the police, who so diligently searched for and apprehended Scott Roeder, who aborted George Tiller, are the same police who protect the men and women who abort little baby boys and girls.

I listened to commentators talking on the news about how we need to "tone down" our rhetoric to avoid violence. What they refuse to see is that our rhetoric is crying out against violence, the violence of child killing. We are the ones who are trying to bring an end to violence and 4,000 murders a day.

I have seen what happens is the past when an abortionist is aborted. The pro-life movement seems to shy away from action. I have seen people drop out of the movement and back away from getting involved.

If anything, we need to step up our fight against violence and the killing of human persons. What this murder showed us is hearts have been hardened to life, and we must shine the light of Christ and hope into this dark world even brighter than ever.

I urge all of you who believe in the sanctity of human life to stay focused. Do not let this despicable act of cowardice sway you from standing up and being a voice for the babies. I know things will be tough, as people will judge us just for being associated with pro-life. We must reiterate that the abortion of George Tiller was not a pro-life act, just as the murder of 4,000 children a day are not pro-life acts.

As for using the term "aborted" when referring to the death of George Tiller, I will stop using that term when the pro-abortion industry starts calling abortion "homicide," which is what it is. I am simply using their own term to describe the taking of a human life; they should have no problem with my using their own language.

21 - Will Our Passion Turn Back to Apathy After the Election?

One of the most positive things I have seen from the 2008 Presidential Election is passion. This election, more than any other I have seen in my time, seems to have brought out a passion in this generation. The unfortunate thing about this is it also sheds light on the apathy that has plagued us for so many years.

Most of my friends know that I am not your typical "right wing voter." I have not voted for a major party for President since 1992. I have always said I vote more for whom or what I believe in, than just to win or beat the other party. I personally don't believe that either of the mainstream political parties truly represents my beliefs very much at all.

This election, for me, is different from any of the other ones I have been involved with. I honestly believe there is more at stake than any other time I can remember, and I have wrestled more than I ever have about whom to vote for. Some may even say I am compromising or being somewhat pragmatic when I never have before.

As much I am not a pragmatist, I have to look at the reality of what could actually happen during an Obama administration. I believe in my heart we could see a devastating attack on life and innocent children like we have never seen before.

Knowing how much this election has troubled me, and how it has affected my vote more than any other, I also see what it has done to this generation. I have seen an awakening of passion, commitment, drive, boldness, and pure excitement that I have not seen before. I have seen this on both sides of the political coin, and I am ecstatic about this. In an age when apathy seems to flow through the veins of America's youth, we are seeing action take over.

I talked to some friends before the election about some of the political talk I had been hearing around town. I told them about people wanting to fly their flag upside down if a certain candidate was elected. You may think that is disrespectful to the flag, but is actually is an accepted signal for a nation in distress. This action is not about disrespect.

I decided to see what kind of reaction I would get if I posted this idea on Facebook. I simply changed my status to a comment about flying the flag upside down and let the fireworks begin. Now, I post a lot of things on Facebook, from contests to "win free stuff" to praise reports about what God has done through our ministry at Stand True. I have also written snippets of travel humor I have encountered when driving 3,000 miles in a van with 10 people. I was guessing this would cause a stir, but I did not think it would reach the fever pitch like when I posted I would be giving away free stickers. Boy, was I wrong.

Just one political comment brought out the passion in everyone, and my status became a heated discussion in no time. I sat and watched people speaking out and engaging in discussion about something that meant so much to them. I got private e-mails from people who thought I was being a bad Christian witness for talking about flying my flag upside down. It was awesome; people were passionate.

I was not and will not tell people who to vote for. But beg each of you to vote. I am not just talking about any specific election. I am talking about your life. I hate the fact that after an election so many people seem to shrink back into their apathy and just ride out the next four years until we get to cast another vote. Why can't this passion and action last past Election Day?

The results of this election had an effect on everyone. Foreign policy, the economy, abortion, health care, and so many more issues are affected by who is in the White House, but one thing did not change. On January 20, 2008, when our new President was inaugurated, one thing remained the same. God was still on the throne, and His sovereignty remained intact. God does not fear any Presidential administration, and He can and will work in our nation no matter who sits in the White House.

No matter who is in the White House, we should not let this passion we have die down. People seem to think that depending on who wins, things like abortion, hunger, poverty, war, or anything we are concerned about will be magically fixed by our President. They will not.

Imagine if we saw the same passion and action we are seeing toward this election being focused on feeding the hungry, giving water to the thirsty, standing for the voiceless, or sharing the Gospel of Christ. What if all the volunteers from all the campaign offices of both parties decided to spend the same amount of time at soup kitchens, homeless shelters, homes for unwed mothers, or youth outreaches? What if the amount of money everyone donated to the candidates was now being donated to charities and ministries?

I want to issue a challenge to everyone who is reading this. Have you volunteered, donated money, or spent time talking to people about either candidate? Why not do the same now that the election is over? Volunteer in your community and make a difference. Donate to a charity or ministry so they can continue to help people. Tell people about getting involved; don't let apathy take over this generation again.

Praying with group at the inauguration of President Obama, Washington DC, 2009

More important than anything else is our passion for Christ. While a President may affect our lives here on earth, it is eternity that is most important. No politician can assure us of anything when it comes to eternity, only Christ's blood can give us the hope we need. Imagine if we had the same passion for sharing the Gospel of Christ as we do for sharing why our candidate is so important.

Deny apathy and embrace passion.

22 - The Cover Up of Child Rape

Over the past nineteen years I have witnessed some of the most grievous and despicable crimes you can imagine. I have spent the last nineteen years of my life dedicated to trying to stop many of these crimes, only to have our government pass laws against my efforts and put me in jail for trying to save lives.

One tactic we used is called "Truth Teams." I would take a young girl into an abortion clinic, and she would ask for a pregnancy test. While I waited for her in the lobby, I would pass out pro-life literature and witness to people in the lobby, and she would fill the back room with pro-life literature. On one occasion I witnessed an abortion take place, and it changed my life forever when I committed to God to do this work until babies were no longer being killed.

While the Truth Teams were effective, and we saw many babies saved and women's lives changed from this outreach, it is no longer possible to do. The government has passed what is called the FACE act, which makes it a federal offense to do outreaches like this.

I recall an occasion back in the '90s that sticks out clearly in my mind. The girl I would take into the abortion mill with me was thirteen-years-old. Her parents would usually wait outside and knew what we were doing. This girl was a virgin

Stand True member sharing at the literature table at the booth, Creation West, Washington, Summer 2009

and had never even kissed a boy in her life, yet twice the abortion mill came out and told us she was pregnant. They were very clear that they would not report us to law enforcement since I was clearly an adult and she was a child. They told us if we paid them in cash, they would do the abortion and not tell anyone.

I know you may be scratching your head right now trying to figure out how a thirteen-year-old virgin who had never even kissed a boy could be pregnant. She obviously wasn't. This fact, however, didn't stop the abortion "doctor" from offering to do an abortion on her (while of course also promising not to report us to the authorities).

I have seen so many mind-blowing things like this over the years, and I wonder how the government continues to ignore and protect this industry. Recently, another video was released of Planned Parenthood willing to protect adult men from having sex and impregnating thirteen-year-old girls. The link to all the video investigations is http://liveaction.org/index.php/projects/monalisa/.

Lila Rose and her organization, Live Action Films, have been going undercover to expose Planned Parenthood for who they truly are. This time they caught a nurse on video telling an investigative reporter posing as a thirteen-year-old girl to lie about her boyfriend's age. She first told her she did not want to know the age, but, after being told he was thirty-one, she told the girl to lie. Recently, Students for Life of America released a similar investigative video showing the same thing (http://www.eyeblast.tv/public/checker.aspx?v=ydprvknz6U).

I get letters back from people often telling me that while they support me in my pro-life views, I am too harsh on the abortion industry. I am told I should not even use terms like "abortion industry" because it unfairly represents medical clinics.

I do not apologize for one second for the way I have and will continue to portray the abortion industry. This is one of the most corrupt and deceitful industries in the world. Even if you took out the fact they are slaughtering almost 4,000 children a day, corruption like we encountered runs deep, and organizations like Planned Parenthood must be stopped.

23 - Planned Parenthood and the Desecration of Christmas

Bryan praying outside Planned Parenthood, St. Louis, Missouri, Summer 2006

As most of the nation celebrates the birth of Christ this Christmas, in Indiana, Planned Parenthood offers gift certificates that can be used for killing your baby. Over the past several years Planned Parenthood has sold "Choice on Earth" Christmas cards and T-shirts each Christmas season. Not only are they raising money to kill babies, the card mocks the birth of Christ.

"Choice on Earth," the name of the Planned Parenthood card, is a disgusting attempt to spread their message of death while exploiting the celebration of the birth of Christ.

"For unto you is born this day in the city of David a Saviour, which is Christ the Lord. And this shall be a sign unto you; Ye shall find the babe wrapped in swaddling clothes, lying in a manger. And suddenly there was with the angel a multitude of the heavenly host praising God, and saying, Glory to God in the highest, and on earth peace, good will toward men" (Luke 2:11-14, KJV).

The phrase "peace on earth" is based on this verse from Holy Scripture. Angels were proclaiming peace on earth, and I am sure no thought of child killing was part of that peace.

What does the word "choice" mean in the context of Planned Parenthood's card? It means abortion. It is the choice to kill your baby through abortion. In essence, Planned Parenthood is celebrating Christmas by saying "abortion on earth." It is ironic that in the day Christ was born, King Herod was having young babies murdered.

King Herod had every boy two years or younger killed because of greed, pride, power, and control. These are also some of the same sins Planned Parenthood will speak to in a young woman to get her to believe she should kill her baby.

Planned Parenthood has become a modern day King Herod. They are more concerned with their own greed than the life of an innocent child.

Their greed and selfishness is more important than life itself.

They make women feel like there is no other choice for their lives but abortion. They instill in them lies about how bad their lives will be if they give birth. They make them fear losing money, control over their own lives, opportunities, and happiness.

Just like King Herod, Planned Parenthood is more concerned about their own wealth, power, and position in life than anything else, and they want to pass that way of thinking onto young women and the world.

They are so dedicated to this evil way of thought, they are willing to mock the birth of Christ and try to steal the true meaning of Christmas.

Christmas is a time of joy and peace as we ponder the birth of our Savior. It is a time to promote love and life, not a time to promote death and hatred.

Planned Parenthood has attempted to steal the meaning of Christmas and distort it as they ignore the very reason we celebrate.

section three

tough questions

Logic 101

A fetus is a human being.

+

Killing a human being is wrong.

+

Abortion is killing a human being.

=

Abortion is wrong.

24 - Pro-Choice or Pro-Abortion: Is There a Difference?

I imagine some people will write and chastise me for the title of this chapter before they even read what I write. It has become very apparent to me that many people don't actually read what is written and consider the points I make. They just like to tell me how wrong I am.

Recently, I wrote a blog in response to the election of Barack Obama, in which I referred to him as "pro-abortion." Some of my readers wrote back to tell me I was hateful for calling him this, or that I was wrong. They claimed he is pro-choice, not pro-abortion. Some even said he is pro-life and wants to do everything he can to reduce abortions.

Before I get into what his agenda is, and why I stand by my words about his position, I want to tackle the pro-abortion or pro-choice argument or "rhetoric"—which is what this really is about.

The rhetoric war has been won for the most part by what I call the pro-abortion movement. They have themselves adopted the term "pro-choice" because it sounds a lot nicer than pro-abortion. I have often wondered why they have not changed another term they use to describe themselves, "abortion rights advocates." If they are pro-choice and not pro-abortion, then why not refer to themselves as "choice rights advocates"?

Let's break down the words and examine what they mean. "Pro" obviously means that you are in support of something. Pro-gun, pro-gay rights, pro-life, pro-union: these are all terms that describe something you support. Why is it then that the term pro-abortion is not used proudly?

The term "pro-choice" should really embody all of the "pro" stances on every issue; it shouldn't just define one issue. When someone refers to themselves as pro-choice, what choice are they referring to? Abortion. So what they are saying is that they believe it is fine for someone to obtain an abortion, which makes them pro-abortion. If you believe people have the right to form and join unions even if you would never join one, you are pro-union. Would you be angry that someone referred to you as pro-union? Would you say I just believe in the choice to join a union, but I am not pro-union? Of course not.

The use of the word *choice* shows that it is all about the stigma of being called pro-abortion. Would there be a stigma if there is nothing wrong with abortion? Why are people so opposed to being referred to as pro-abortion if abortion is perfectly acceptable?

Bryan speaking at a teen pro-life conference, Philadelphia, Summer 2007

To answer that, we have to determine what abortion is. Is abortion simply the termination of a pregnancy? Is abortion just a medical procedure that removes unwanted cell masses from your body, something equated with liposuction?

The answer to those questions is a resounding "no." Abortion is the termination of a pregnancy, but what is a pregnancy? The Merriam-Webster Dictionary definition of *pregnant* reads: "containing a developing embryo, fetus, or unborn offspring within the body."[1]

Abortion is the termination or killing of a developing human person in the early stages of their life. It is that simple. We can try and sanitize it with words or phrases, but that does not change what it is.

There are a lot of things that are unpleasant that people or organizations try to make less appalling by changing the words used to describe them. As a parent, I am guilty of this myself. When my children need to defecate I do not use that term. I say, "Go potty." Does this change the fact that they are defecating?

<hr />

[1]Merriam-Webster's Collegiate ® Dictionary 11th Edition ©2009 by Merriam-Webster, Incorporated www.Merriam-Webster.com

No, it just makes it sound less gross and nasty.

That is why the pro-abortion movement wants to be referred to as pro-choice, not pro-abortion. Abortion carries a stigma with which they don't want to be identified. The difference is there is nothing wrong with defecating. It is natural and how our bodies were created to work. There is, however, something wrong with abortion. It is unnatural and destroys one of the natural functions of a woman's body.

We should not give in to the sanitization of abortion. It needs to be exposed for what it is. We should not allow rhetoric to define how we describe an evil like the killing of innocent persons.

I have often heard pro-abortion people say they would love to see abortion reduced or minimized. Why? If there is nothing immoral or wrong about abortion, then why would we care how many people have them? Why would we want to reduce something that is perfectly OK? If you want to reduce them, then you must think there is something wrong with them. What is wrong?

Barack Obama tries to sound like he is not the pro-abortion advocate that he really is. His own words and record contradict that. What he does as President will be dangerous and devastating to this nation and the world.

In the first week we heard he reversed lifesaving Executive Orders that will result in the destruction of human life worldwide. He plans to reverse the "Mexico City Policy" which blocks the US Government from giving money to organizations who provide abortion in other countries. We are now paying for abortions overseas with our tax dollars. He opened up the funding of destruction of human embryos for research paid for with your tax dollars.

This is just the beginning of the destruction of human life that has been and will continue to be championed by Barack Obama. During the primary season he spoke at a Planned Parenthood event and promised that one of the first things he would do as President is sign the FOCA bill into law. The Freedom of Choice Act would wipe out all restrictions on abortion in this country. There will be no more parental notification, no restrictions whatsoever including the Partial Birth Abortion Ban and an increase in federal funding of abortion.

How can you say you want to reduce abortions, then wipe out every restriction there is and fund abortion in the US and other countries with US tax dollars? The pro-life movement and, more importantly, the sanctity of human life has been set back over thirty years now that Barack Obama has taken the office of President.

I have been told that speaking negatively about the President is hateful and disrespectful. I have been told I need to support our new President and just pray for him. I agree that we need to pray for him, and pray hard. I, however, disagree that pointing out the truth of what he has done, and has promised to do, is hateful in any way. I would even argue that silence would be hateful. Apathy and acceptance of his plans would be disrespectful to those whose lives are in jeopardy.

I know God is still on the throne, and He is sovereign. I know God is not worried, panicking, or hiding in a corner in fear. I know that He is still our King, and our only hope is in His Son, Jesus.

I also know that He commands us to "love thy neighbor as thyself" (Luke 10:27, KJV). When our neighbors are dying by the thousands every day in this nation, we have an obligation to stand up and fight for their lives. God calls us to "rescue those being led away to death; hold back those staggering toward slaughter" (Proverbs 24:11, NIV).

I will not cheapen the sanctity of life or sanitize the pro-abortion movement by using the term pro-choice. I will not sit by quietly as my brothers and sisters are being slaughtered in abortion mills every day. I will pray for, but not support, our President as he opens the floodgates and destroys all regulations and restrictions against the killing of innocent children.

To say you are pro-choice but not pro-abortion, is simply illogical.

25 - Christians Should Be Proselytizing, Not Politicizing

I cannot tell you how many pastors throw this argument at me as an excuse for not getting involved with pro-life work or even talking about it from the pulpit. It actually surprises me that a pastor would even try to justify his apathy and lack of involvement in standing up for life.

Obviously we all know as Christians our main focus is to spread the Gospel and share the hope we have in Christ. We are commanded to "go ye into all the world and preach the Gospel to every creature" (Mark 16:15, KJV).

Approximately fifty teens from Apex Community Church praying outside abortion mill, Kettering, Ohio, Summer 2007

I remember one pastor in particular who told me that I had no business telling anyone abortion was wrong. He said I should only tell people about Jesus and nothing else. I laid out a situation for him to answer using his logic. What if you came upon a man beating a woman in an alley? Would you walk up to the man, tap him on the shoulder, and tell him about Jesus, or would you first stop the man from beating the woman and make sure she was taken care of?

He tried to wiggle out of answering the question at first but eventually said he would first stop the man from harming the woman and make sure she was OK. I asked him why he would not just tell the man about Jesus and not worry about his behavior. He said because the woman was in imminent danger and needed to be rescued.

The fact is we are also called in scripture to "rescue those being led away to death; hold back those staggering toward slaughter. If you say, 'But we knew nothing about this,' does not he who weighs the heart perceive it?" (Proverbs 24:11-12, NIV).

We are also called to "love the Lord your God with all your heart and with all your soul and with all your strength and with all your mind," and, to "love thy neighbor as thyself" (Luke 10:27, KJV).

The church cannot be excused for apathy and a lack of involvement when it comes to abortion. We have allowed the government to politicize abortion to the point that we just don't pay attention any more. We are more than happy to let our votes on Election Day be the only action we ever take as we leave it up to politicians who don't always deliver on their promises.

Preaching the Gospel is not just leaving cheesy Bible tracts with a lousy tip on the table at Applebee's after church. Preaching the Gospel is not just saying "Jesus loves you" to your friends at work after laughing at all their dirty jokes. Preaching the Gospel goes far beyond our words and must also include action. Feeding the poor, giving water to the thirsty, and speaking up for the voiceless *is* preaching the Gospel.

26 - What Would the Punishment Be If Abortion Were Illegal?

This is probably one of the toughest questions to answer as a pro-lifer. I will try to answer this from a pro-life perspective that won't anger too many people. I have had this discussion with many people who have solid pro-life views, yet are confused as to how they feel about the laws and punishment when it comes to abortion. People ask me what legally happens to the women and doctors if we overturn Roe v. Wade.

My first response is that the end goal of the pro-life movement is not overturning Roe v. Wade. We absolutely want that to happen, however that is only the first step. Overturning this Supreme Court decision will only send the issue back to the individual states to pass laws. Most likely any law passed by a state will then be challenged in court and end up right back at the Supreme Court.

The end goal is to establish that life begins at the moment of fertilization. This will only be achieved with a paramount Human Life Amendment to the Constitution. With a Human Life Amendment we can establish the starting point in a human person's life that cannot be challenged by any court. This will give children in the womb the same rights and protections under the Constitution as any other human person.

This is where the dilemma of the question begins. Do you truly believe that a child in the womb is a fully human person? Do you believe that the unborn child is equal in value to a three-year-old child playing on a playground? As a pro-life advocate, I do not see how you could answer no to either of those questions.

The core of the pro-life argument is that every single human person from fertilization to natural death should be protected. If we say the child in the womb is a human person and their life is already begun, then how can we say they should not be protected equally?

The problem comes when we look at this from the wrong direction. Whenever I debate someone who is defending abortion, the first thing they try to do is direct the argument onto rabbit trails. They bring up all of the emotional situations and try to only argue from the extreme cases. They do this because they know if they can tug the heartstrings of those in the audience, they can sway them and distract them from the truth. They try and steer away from the core of the issue: the personhood of the child, which is the point we need to keep the argument on.

The same thing happens when I discuss the issue of punishment for abortion with pro-lifers. They talk about the desperate woman who knows it is illegal but can't afford her baby. They ask if she should really be punished for making a hard decision. We have no way of knowing what is going on in her life or what she is going through.

I admit there is an emotional element to this that can blur the issue. I know that no one wants to put thousands of women in prison. It is sincerely a tough question.

Let's change the direction from which we look at this, however. Just like in my debates against pro-abortion advocates, I would steer away from the distractions and focus on the core issue. What is abortion? Abortion is the killing of a human person. Just like stabbing a three-year-old on a playground is killing a human person, stabbing a baby in the womb is also killing a human person.

Bryan's third child, Madilynn, sharing one of the fetal models with team member, Purple Door, Lewisberry, Pennsylvania, Summer 2006

If we establish a "Human Life Amendment" to the Constitution declaring that children are full human persons from the moment of fertilization, then we must treat them as such.

When the Susan Smith drowned her two children several years ago, what was your thought on her punishment? Did you believe because she had some rough times at home she should be excused from what she did? The fact is, she killed her two children and had to answer to the law. While we might feel sorry for her emotional state, we must also want justice for the children who were killed.

In the same way, we must look at the children in the womb as equal in value to the children who were drowned and demand justice for them also. We can certainly feel empathy for what a woman might be going through, however, that cannot change the fact that she broke the law and ended the life of her child.

If we make a separate law and separate punishment for someone who has an abortion, then we are saying the child in the womb is somehow not as valuable as any other human person killed. If we say intentionally killing one child is less of a crime than intentionally killing another child, then our whole argument for life is destroyed.

I know many of you are probably upset right now or even confused about what you think. I understand completely. I have spent twenty years thinking about this question and going over every possible way to look at it. The one constant I always come back to is the fundamental right to life of every human person.

I may not have an answer for what the punishment should be, I'll leave that up to the judicial system. But I do know we must protect all human persons including those in the womb. I don't want to define a specific punishment for this particular act of homicide, because I don't want to separate it from every other act of homicide. The fact is, the killing of a human person is already punishable by law and the killing of a child in the womb should fall under those same laws.

27 - The Argument: "I am Against Abortion, but it Should Remain Legal so it is Safe"

People argue that even if we are successful in outlawing abortion, it will continue regardless of the law, so these people argue that we need to keep it legal so it can be safe. This is one of the arguments I hear most from people who don't want to get involved in pro-life work. It is also one of the most absurd arguments I have ever heard.

DCLA, Washington DC, Summer 2006

The very premise of the argument discounts the reason we are against abortion. It kills a human person. How can abortion ever be thought of as safe? The very act of abortion destroys the life of an innocent child. Where is the safety in that?

If you follow this logic you can carry it to ludicrous lengths. You can argue burglary is illegal, yet it happens anyway so why don't we make it legal so criminals can have a safer time committing this crime. You can argue that rape is illegal, yet it happens anyway, so we should open clinics where someone can commit that crime safely.

These are obviously insane arguments that don't make sense. The same is true for saying that killing children through abortion will happen no matter what so we need to keep clinics open for people to commit that crime.

This question is really not that tough at all. We have laws to protect people from being harmed by other people.

[2]Merriam-Webster's Collegiate ® Dictionary 11th Edition ©2009 by Merriam-Webster, Incorporated www.Merriam-Webster.com

Merriam-Webster Dictionary defines homicide as "a killing of one human being by another" or "a person who kills another."[2]

Imagine if we changed the definition of homicide to look like this: "the killing of one person by another, except when done in a safe medical clinic because someone did not want to take care of the other person," or "a person who kills another person, except when the first person is a doctor who is paid to kill that person" (Bryan's Ridiculous Dictionary).

Abortion is the killing of one person by another person; therefore it is homicide and should be illegal. It is that simple.

28 - If Abortion is a Women's Issue, Should Men Stay Out of It?

I often get e-mails and messages telling me that I should stay out of the "abortion issue" because I'm a man. I've been told I have no business getting involved since I can never get pregnant.

The problem with this argument is that it's meant to detract from the key issue of personhood. Most arguments you will hear from the pro-abortion side are simply rabbit trails meant to steer clear of personhood, the heart of what we are fighting for.

The first mistake anyone can make is to refer to it as the "abortion issue." While abortion is the largest part of the personhood fight, it is still just one part of the culture of death and the destruction of personhood.

This is not just about women either. It's about everyone involved, including the mother, the father, and the baby. To think that the mother of the child being killed is the only one who has any right to an opinion is absurd. Unfortunately, this argument is often used by men who call themselves pro-life. They say that, while they are pro-life, they have no business telling a woman not to kill her child.

Imagine if the rest of the world had that same attitude during the Nazi Holocaust. "We are not German so we have no right telling them not to kill other people." That is an insane argument, no one could agree with a statement like that. To know about the killing of innocent human persons and do nothing about it because it was "none of your business"? How absurd.

As we came into the 21st century it became extremely popular to stand up and be a voice for conflicts like the one in Darfur. (If you are not familiar with what is happening in Darfur, I highly encourage you to look into the genocide that is happening there and so many other regions of the world. A great film to watch is *Invisible Children*. You can also find a good brief history on Wikipedia.) Should we tell people to mind their own business because we're not from there, and therefore have no right to an opinion? Or should we not be worried about the blatant human rights violations going on in China simply because we are not Chinese?

Edmund Burke, an Irish orator, philosopher and politician, once said, "All that is necessary for the triumph of evil is that good men do nothing." The evil of killing children has triumphed in America for over 35 years now. This triumph has been fueled by the apathy and denial of this generation.

Have you noticed how popular superhero movies are? We love to see Spider-man or Batman take out the bad guys as we cheer them on from the sidelines. We teach our kids that crime doesn't pay and make heroes out of those who fight against evil. I wonder what kind of lesson we teach them when we ourselves ignore evil because it's "none of our business"?

Bryan sharing with teens at the literature table, Creation West, George, Washington, Summer 2009

We know what is happening in abortion mills and doctors' offices every day. We know that little baby boys and girls are being destroyed in the name of choice as we turn a blind eye. Some people are waiting for the politicians to step up, as if they are going to be like Superman and swoop down to rescue the children right before the doctor's suction machine destroys them.

Well, as a father, I refuse to wait for some superhero or politician to teach my child a lesson about what is right and wrong. I refuse to tell my kids that they should take a stand against evil and fight for justice while I sit by and ignore the genocide that is killing one third of their generation.

As a man, as a father, and as a human I will not stay out of the "abortion issue." As human persons, we cannot look at abortion simply as a women's issue. We must see it for what it is: the killing of innocent human persons. We should not get involved because we are men or women, but because we are human, and it is our fellow human persons who are facing genocide.

29 – Abortion is Not Mentioned in The Bible

I got an email the other day asking me about abortion and the Bible. This is actually a question I have gotten quite a bit. Abortion is not mentioned in the Bible, so how can we say it is a sin?

This question is flawed because it is focused on the procedure rather than what abortion actually is. That is one of the fundamental reasons Christians ignore abortion, they look at it as a procedure. We must look past the procedure to the root of what abortion is: murder.

There are many ways to kill a human person, and not all of them are mentioned in the Bible. Using this logic, you could argue that shooting someone with a gun is not mentioned in the Bible, therefore, it is not a sin. Shooting someone with a gun, like abortion, is simply the procedure used to kill that human person.

We all know that killing an innocent person is a sin, "Thou shalt not commit murder" is pretty cut and dry.

Bryan going over the weekend schedule with the group at the March for Life 2009, Washington DC

Scripture tells us about the beginning of human life. I am sure you have all heard the most popular verse pro-lifers use about God forming us in the womb. Then read Psalm 51:5 (KJV), "Behold, I was brought forth in iniquity, And in sin my mother conceived me." From the moment of conception you have sin. What does sin stain? It stains your soul, not your flesh. You have a soul at the moment of conception.

Let's look at Luke 1:39-45 (NIV), "At that time Mary got ready and hurried to a town in the hill country of Judea, where she entered Zechariah's home and greeted Elizabeth. When

Elizabeth heard Mary's greeting, the baby leaped in her womb, and Elizabeth was filled with the Holy Spirit. In a loud voice she exclaimed: "Blessed are you among women, and blessed is the child you will bear! But why am I so favored, that the mother of my Lord should come to me? As soon as the sound of your greeting reached my ears, the baby in my womb leaped for joy. Blessed is she who has believed that what the Lord has said to her will be accomplished!"

Elizabeth was pregnant with John the Baptist and was about six months along in her pregnancy. Mary was only a few days pregnant with Jesus when John the Baptist recognized the personhood of Christ and leapt in the womb. It cannot be any clearer when life begins.

So again it comes back to the core of the pro-life argument: personhood.

That was the long answer to the question. The short answer is simple. Abortion is mentioned in the Bible. "Thou shalt not commit murder."

30 - Situational Abortion

Every year Stand True hosts an event called the Pro-life Day of Silent Solidarity in which students around the world take a vow of silence in solidarity with the children who have been killed by abortion. In 2009, when this book was written, over fifty girls that we know of cancelled abortions because of this event. One of the questions I get asked the most from students participating in this event is about situational abortions.

"What if the girl was raped? What if she was poor and the baby was going to have a hard life?" The problem with these questions is they are looking at situations rather than the core of the issue, personhood. These are arguments for the procedure of abortion that ignore the personhood of the child.

While all of these situations can be heart-wrenching and abortion seems to be the logical option, they have to be weighed against the core truth of personhood. Every single child from the moment of fertilization is a full human person. We cannot take the life of an innocent human person, and, therefore, these are not valid arguments for the procedure of abortion.

Stand True member sharing fetal model at the booth, Creation West, George Washington, Summer 2009

I especially wonder how so many Christians can support these situational arguments. We have the ultimate truth in the Word of God to guide us in questions like these. The Bible clearly states, "Thou shalt not commit murder." There are no exceptions written next to that commandment, no footnotes that claim in highly emotional cases it is okay. It is a command.

When we talk about abortion, we must always bring it back to the core issue, personhood. If the child in the womb was not a human person, abortion would not matter. The child is, however, a human person, and, therefore, must be afforded all rights as a human person. If we say that in certain circumstances abortion is OK, then we are saying that there are times when the child is not a human person. That is simply not the case.

31 – My Friend is Pregnant and Considering Abortion

Many young people have said to me, "What do I say to my pregnant friend? Is it my place to say anything to her?" This is probably one of the hardest questions I have to answer, and unfortunately it is asked too often. I have talked to countless women who were considering abortion. I wish I could tell you that I was able to talk all of them out of an abortion, but I can't. There are no magic words you can say that will automatically change someone's mind. There is no set answer that will work in every situation.

We have to consider several things in order to answer this question. First, we need to address our own hearts, and how we react to someone who comes to us in this situation.

I can tell you from my own experience that in my early years, I turned many people from pro-life work with my own actions. I used my knowledge and passion to attack those who did not agree with me. I spoke without thinking about the words I was saying, and hurt people I was trying to reach. While I was trying to love the baby, I forgot to love the mother I was also trying to reach.

In order to talk to a friend about this, we must first be ready to listen. We must be able to understand what our friend is going through and be able to talk about her problems and needs. Just convincing her that her baby is really a baby does not take away whatever brought her to this decision.

Then it comes time to talk to our friend about the life of the child in her womb. We must never approach this in a situational way. So many people think that the situation someone is in defines the level of personhood of the child. There are no *levels of* personhood; there is *only* personhood. We must establish the personhood of the child in the womb. Here is a good example of proving life or personhood begins at conception.

Ask someone if they know when we stop growing and developing as humans. The answer is at death. Our ears and nose grow until the day we die. If you take that backward to a starting point, you can only come up with one precise moment that growth and development start: conception. So each stage of life: zygote, embryo, fetus, infant, toddler, teen, adult, senior; are all just that: stages of human life.

We must also be knowledgeable about life and what life is. If we cannot answer basic questions about the life of the child, then how can we expect someone to trust us or listen to us? In situations like this, I would highly encourage you to take your friend to a pregnancy resource center to talk to a trained counselor. Many of these centers have doctors and nurses on staff and even free ultrasound machines. You can always call 1-800-395-HELP, and they will connect you to the center closest to you.

Stand True member sharing at the booth, Alive Festival, Canal Fulton, Ohio, Summer 2006

While getting your friend to a pregnancy resource center would be the best option, many times they won't want to talk to anyone else. In a situation like this you can always call us at Stand True (937) 339-5648 or email us at info@standtrue.com and we can get you the resources you need to help your friend. We would be happy to mail you literature, fetal models or any other resource you need to talk to your friend. Our contact information can be found on our web site, www.**standtrue**.com, and there are a lot of resources for you under the "Educate Yourself" section.

This would bring us to the second half of the question, "Is it my place to say anything to her?" One of the most common things I hear from people is they don't want to push their beliefs on someone else. Though they believe abortion is wrong, they worry that it's not their place to tell anyone else that it is.

Some people believe it is OK to beat their children or beat their wives. An actual organization, "NAMBLA," believes it is OK for grown men to have sexual relations with young boys, truly believes that it is okay. I would ask someone who did not like to push their beliefs on someone else if they would ignore a man beating his wife. Would they look the other way if a man were going to harm a young boy?

If the child in the womb is a human person, then we have an obligation to stand up for their life. It is not a question of pushing your beliefs on someone, but a matter of loving our neighbor as our self.

With all of this said, I would also encourage you to pray for your friend and offer her prayer. Even if she were not a Christian, many women would welcome prayer in a rough situation. Prayer is the most powerful tool that we have, and it works. After all, it's not really you who will change your friend's heart; it is God.

Please feel free to ask us for prayer in these situations also. You can always e-mail me directly and ask for prayer bryankemper@standtrue.com.

You can also call 1-800-395-HELP for some advice in talking to your friend.

section four

reflections on god

Hate, Love; Satan, Jesus

Hate, deep,
Penetrating through the heart
Like a piercing arrow.
Blind, without bias,
Striking anywhere
With devastating accuracy.

Love, deep,
Healing the broken heart
With total **peace**.
Blind, without bias,
With you everywhere,
With unfailing devotion.

Satan, **hate**,
Poisoning the heart
Like a venomous snake.
Blind, without bias,
Luring you to death
To die for Him.

Jesus, **love**,
Healing the heart
Like a peaceful dove.
Blind, without bias,
Giving you eternal **life**.
He died for you.

32 - A Joyful Noise

The other night I was invited to a home Bible study with some people from Bethany Christian Services and the Fredericksburg, VA local food bank. As we started to sing a few praise songs, I could not help but notice the woman to my left. She was an older woman who was somewhat hard of hearing. As she began to sing, she was almost a second or two off from everyone else and way off key. At first it kind of threw me off, but as I looked at her and saw the smile on her face as she sang to God, it really touched me. She did not need to be on key and she did not need to be in perfect time with everyone. She just needed to make a joyful noise unto God.

This made me think back to my days with Youth With A Mission (YWAM) and our outreach to the Cook Islands. Our missionary team did a lot of dramas and singing. While most of the team were very good singers, I had a voice that made people cringe. The team leader got so frustrated with me that he actually asked me to just lip-sync while the rest of the group sang. I quietly obliged. However, it really made me sad, especially when we sang praise songs.

I think sometimes Christians can focus on all the wrong things. I see kids trying so hard to convince everyone that everything is OK when they are hurting inside and ready to explode. They don't want their parents or youth pastor to know that they have struggles with sin, because they think that would mean they aren't good Christians. Instead of seeking help and support, they turn to drugs, alcohol, sex, abortion, and suicide to be able to cope with their problems.

This is especially true with young girls who get pregnant out of wedlock. It seems that once this happens, everyone sees them as a leper, and parents tell their kids not to hang out with "that pregnant girl." I can't tell you how many times I have talked to kids whose parents forced them into abortion to avoid having to face society and the church because they "failed as parents." I have seen pastors take their daughters into abortion clinics because they are more concerned about losing their church than the welfare of their daughter and grandchild.

I know that as a father with daughters, I am going to have to face some of these problems in the future. While I try to teach my children about chastity, respecting themselves, and pray for them, I know they still will sin. They may not get pregnant or do drugs, but they will face tough times and struggle, as all humans do. I pray that in those days I will have the courage to embrace my children and love them, no matter what the situation.

We have to remember that without Christ we are all filthy with sin. The Bible says, "But we are all like an unclean thing, And all our righteousnesses are like filthy rags; We all fade as a leaf, And our iniquities, like the wind, Have taken us away. There is nothing we can do to make ourselves clean. We can only turn to Christ and be cleansed by His blood. It is Him who makes us clean and Him alone" (Isaiah 64:6, KJV).

No matter what we are going through, we can go to Christ, confess our sins, and He is faithful to forgive us. He comforts us when we are broken and loves us when we are unlovable. "If we confess our sins, he is faithful and just and will forgive us our sins and purify us from all unrighteousness" (1 John 1:9, KJV).

Why, then, can't we treat others like this? Why is it when our brothers and sisters in Christ are hurting and struggling, we look down on them and act as if we are better than them? Do we not remember that, without Christ, we are all filthy?

When a young woman sins and gets pregnant, should we treat her like a leper or a disease? If we do, then we are just going to push her further down the path toward abortion. Is her sin somehow so bad that we can't imagine loving her and being there for her to help her find forgiveness and comfort with Christ?

If you have the best voice in the world and sing to God, while the person next to you has the worse voice ever and also sings to God, both of you are making a joyful noise unto the Lord God, who hears both of your voices as beautiful. He takes delight in His children singing praises to Him and does not care if their voices are off key.

If we can all come to God equally with all of our imperfections, then should we not be able to come to each other and seek love from God's people, no matter what we are struggling with? We must stop killing our own wounded and love them, because, in all reality, we are all wounded without Christ. Maybe then we can put all of our defenses down and throw away all of our cover-ups, truly seeking God, and make a joyful noise to Him without caring what anyone thinks.

Noah, from the band Pillar, wearing Stand True's "silenced" t-shirt on stage, Kingdom Bound, New York, Summer 2006

"Make a joyful noise unto the LORD, all the earth: make a loud noise, and rejoice, and sing" (Psalm 98:4, KJV).

33 - Tearing Up Carpet

Bryan and his three sons: Jaemison, Atticus, and Emmerich, Troy, Ohio, July 2009

In 2007 Stand True and my family moved to Troy, Ohio. We bought a very old house in Troy that would fit my family and the Stand True offices and missionaries. In Ohio you can get almost four times the house for your money that you can in Virginia.

So, my wife and I woke up one Sunday morning to the sounds of our two-year-old, Jaemison, throwing up on me and the carpet next to the bed. After taking care of Jaemison, my wife and I went back to bed. When we woke up, we noticed a bad stench and huge stains in the carpet despite my wife's attempt to clean it earlier. Unfortunately, the carpet was holding the stains and the smell.

My wife pulled up the vent near the stains and let out a yell because she realized that under the smelly, stained carpet were beautiful, old hardwood floors. Over the next few days, we actually pulled up the carpet in the living room, dining room, and a lot of the upstairs only to find some of the most amazing and beautiful hardwood floors we had ever seen.

While the hardwood has some imperfections from old furniture and years of living, it is absolutely beautiful. In fact, the imperfections and wear spots give it a lot of character. We have decided we want to leave it how it is and enjoy the character of the wood and the years of stories it tells about our house.

Many times we, as humans, try to mask who we really are. We think that the imperfections we have make us less valuable or less attractive. We "lay down carpet" to cover up the real people, to hide our true character.

I understand why we do that. Because so many people focus in on our imperfections and wear spots, and we ourselves often look at people, notice their rough edges and make judgments on those alone. We don't see the whole person and understand that we all have imperfections. We just want to point those things out in others and ignore the fact that we have just as many if not a whole lot more.

It is no wonder people try to hide and cover who they really are. It is no wonder people don't want to share when they are struggling or going through hard times. I meet kids all the time who are so angry at the church because, when they did open up, they were devoured instead of loved and helped. I meet kids that are so hurt and lost inside because they are afraid to let anyone know they are struggling with sin. It seems so many in the church would rather just "lay down more carpet" to cover up our problems so that no one knows they are there. The problem is the smell doesn't go away.

People are afraid that if anyone knew that Christians struggle just like everyone else, then we might get called hypocrites. But it is the very act of covering up the struggles with a pretty exterior and pretending that they don't exist that makes us hypocrites, especially when that cover is ripped away, and we are exposed for who we really are.

We seem to think that we have to impress everyone around us to show them how together we are...now that we're Christians. The fact is, we are still imperfect humans with struggles and problems just like anyone else. We can't make ourselves perfect. It is only Christ who can perfect us.

Maybe if Christians were to live their lives without all the fancy cover-ups and just be real with each other, then the world might actually see the beauty of Christ and what He can do. Not just a bunch of fake, happy people who pretend not to struggle or sin. Not the bunch of self-righteous hypocrites as the world often thinks of us.

Of course we are happy, and we are filled with the joy of Christ. Of course we are made new and washed clean by His blood. But we are still human, and we will still go through human struggles while we are on this earth.

Maybe if we were willing to look past those imperfections in others, we would be able to love them and help them to find that victory and freedom we have in Christ. Maybe if we "pulled back the carpet" in our own lives, we would be able to be there to love our brothers and sisters who are so afraid to open up because they think no one can possibly be as screwed up as them.

I would think that if, at any given moment, we could actually see what was in the minds and hearts of all of our friends; we would be shocked. I am talking about the innermost thoughts that we all hide away. We would be surprised to see that we all go through some of the same struggles and sins.

We all run this race that we call life, and we are all going to fall down and scrape and bruise ourselves along the way. But we must press on toward that goal, that hope we have received through Christ.

"Not that I have already obtained all this, or have already been made perfect, but I press on to take hold of that for which Christ Jesus took hold of me. Brothers, I do not consider myself yet to have taken hold of it. But one thing I do: Forgetting what is behind and straining toward what is ahead, I press on toward the goal to win the prize for which God has called me heavenward in Christ Jesus (Philippians 3:12-14, NIV).

34 - Jesus Said

Jesus said: "I am the way, and the truth, and the life. No one comes to the father except through me" (John 14:6, NIV). Think about that for a minute, it is a pretty bold statement. In fact, it can be taken as downright offensive. By saying this, Jesus is basically saying that any other claims of any other religions are false and will not lead you to heaven. He is claiming to be the only true means of salvation.

Can a claim like that fit in with today's climate of tolerance and acceptance? Can we truly go around and teach that any other teaching or religion is false? Can we actually tell people that they cannot get to heaven but through Christ?

Absolutely!

It seems people are more afraid of offending others than of telling them the truth. It is more important to make them feel comfortable and accepted, so we water down the Gospel. We seem to think that we are the ones to save people, so we manipulate the truth and give it every twist we can to fit into today's culture.

Popular or not, the Bible is the truth, and Christ's claim to being the only way to the Father is true and nothing can change that. Will people be offended? Yes. Should we change what we teach and believe because of that? No.

I am not sure where the thought that Christ never offended people came from, but it is far from the truth. I don't know how anyone can think it is up to us to save people, and we need to make the Gospel "cool" or "modern" to fit today's culture. Jesus is the same today, yesterday, and forever. He is relevant to today without our having to dress Him up or soften His message.

If you don't want to offend people, then you probably better not read the Bible to anyone. If you don't want to offend people, you probably better not teach the Gospel. If you don't want to offend people in your church, you should probably replace the parables and teachings of Christ with nice fluffy stories and analogies. If you don't want to offend people, then you should definitely not get involved with Stand True.

We do not set out to offend. Our being offensive is very different from the offense of the Gospel. We want to set out to proclaim the truth that Jesus is the way, and the truth, and the life (John 14:6, NIV). We will proclaim that no one will come to the Father, but through Him. We will proclaim that the killing of

Bryan hanging out with friends at the Stand True booth, Cornerstone Festival, Illinois, Summer 2007

innocent children in the womb is murder. We will proclaim that the Ten Commandments were actually commandments and not suggestions. While our goal is not to offend, if we are not offending, then we are probably not doing our job.

35 - My Three-Year-Old Son, God, and Peanuts

My office is in my home, which is great in some ways. One of the best parts of having my office at home is the amount of time I get to see my family: my kids love coming into the office to show me their home school work or art projects. Of course, they also come to me when one of their siblings upsets them, which in a family of five kids can add up sometimes.

Bryan and his fourth child, Jaemison, at Steak 'n Shake, Ohio, Summer 2008

Lately my three-year-old son, Jaemison, has been coming in with the cutest look on his face to tell me how much he loves me. "Hi Daddy, I love you," is enough to melt the toughest man's heart. But once I look down at him to give him love, he proceeds with the next line, "Daddy, I'm hungry."

It took me a couple of times to figure out that he knew exactly what he was doing. He had figured out that I like to keep a jar of peanuts on my desk, and he loves peanuts. He knows that if he butters me up, I will be much more sympathetic to his request for some peanuts.

Even though I know exactly what he is up to, I always give him a handful of peanuts. He may think he has somehow tricked me into giving him the peanuts, but I do it because I love him, and I want him to be happy.

Isn't it funny how we sometimes do this with our Father in heaven? I have noticed that sometimes when I am praying for something, I seem to be extra repentant or lay it on thick, as if that was going to make God more sympathetic to my prayers.

At church we have communion every Sunday, which I love so much. But I find it funny that on Saturday night and Sunday morning, I am more aware of my thoughts, words, and actions because of communion. Somehow I think because it is so close to communion time, I need to watch myself more. I always question myself and ask why I don't have the same sense of urgency and reverence on Monday morning.

I have always held the belief that I will not lie to my children for any reason. I will not tell them Santa Claus exists so they better behave or they won't get any gifts. I will not tell them a certain food is something else to get them to eat it. I just want to be honest with them.

I want to instill in them a desire to be totally honest with me. I want them to know they never need to manipulate me in any way. They can just come to me with whatever is on their minds. I don't want them to try to be extra good just because they want or need something. I want them to be good because it is the right thing to do. I want them to tell me they love me just because they do, not to get something.

(As I am writing this, my son just came in to get some peanuts. This time he sat on my lap and asked me questions about stuff on my desk, and then pointed to the peanuts.)

So my question to myself and all of you is simple: do you change the way you talk to God when you want something from Him? Do you suddenly act more contrite in your prayers? Do you pour on the "Christian buzz words" to make your prayers seem more sincere?

I will be honest, sometimes I do. Just like my son wanting some peanuts, I sometimes think I have to butter Him up to show how much I really want or need something.

God knows our hearts; He sees right through all of our garbage. I don't believe He wants us to clean up our acts just because something special is coming up. He wants us to clean up our acts because He loves us and wants the best for us. He wants us to talk to Him with straightforward honesty. He wants the real us.

I don't give my son peanuts just because he sits on my lap and warms my heart. I give my son peanuts because he likes them, and I love him. I still want him to come and sit on my lap and tell me he loves me. I still want him to warm my heart. I just want him to do that because he loves me, not just to get some peanuts.

In the same way, God wants us to come into His presence and praise Him, not just when we need something, but also because we love Him.

36 – What Shines Through Us?

I was looking out the kitchen window last week while making my breakfast. I was thinking about how beautiful it was to see the sun shining after recently having such cold and wet weather. As I looked into the backyard, I noticed part of the ground was wet, and it looked like it was raining in half of the yard. I looked up to see it was ice melting off of a big tree, and little icicles were falling off the tree as the sun was melting them.

A few weeks ago, I remember driving home from the store and commenting on how the branches of the trees were really starting to bend and droop under the weight of the ice. While the tree in my yard looked kind of cool with all the icicles, it was not different from any other tree in the neighborhood. They were all covered in ice.

I went out later that night and saw the tree again. While all the trees in the neighborhood still just looked like trees covered in ice, the tree in front of my house really caught my eye. The streetlight was right behind the branches, and the light was shining through all of the icicles. It was an amazing sight to see as the light illuminated the ice and almost brought the icicles to life. I stood and stared at the tree. I had never seen it look so amazing. The light shining through and illuminating the ice was truly beautiful.

I looked around the neighborhood and thought about how much of a difference the light made. I thought about people, and how, when we let the light of Christ shine through us, it makes such a difference. I wondered about how people see me in a crowd of other people. Do they just see me as one of many, or do they see the light of Christ shining through me?

Unfortunately, the answer to that question is not always "Yes." I know at times I don't stand in the light of Christ, but instead follow the ways of the world. The light is always there, I just allow myself to get in the way.

One of the arguments I hear so often against Christianity is not actually against Christianity, but against the behavior and actions of Christians. People have such a hard time listening to us because we don't live what we claim to believe as truth. I realize no one is perfect, but that seems to be a safety net we thought out to justify actions that counter our belief.

Likewise, I also think it's funny how much time we spend trying to make ourselves look good physically, yet we fail to think about what our words do to make us look like idiots. We try on clothes before we buy them to make sure they fit and look right, but will we think about what we are going to say before we open our mouths and hurt someone?

We will take showers, brush our teeth, and put on clean clothes so we don't smell and offend people around us. We make sure our hair is done and our clothes match so we don't look like fools when we walk out of the house. I wonder what would happen if we spent that much time trying to cleanse our minds and hearts every day. Imagine if we made sure our words and interactions with people matched what we claim to stand for and believe.

We will work out our bodies by going to the gym or taking walks, but will we spend the same amount of time exercising our faith? We might look at what ingredients are in the food we eat and care about what we put into our bodies, but we will allow total garbage to enter our hearts and minds. We filter our water before drinking it, yet allow our hearts and minds to be contaminated by what we watch on television.

The sight of the light shining through that tree was amazing and beautiful. While there were many trees covered in ice up and down my street, it was the one illuminated by the light that really moved me. There are many of us who call ourselves Christians and claim to represent our Savior. So many

Stand True team praying outside Planned Parenthood, Boston, Summer 2006

times we let ourselves just blend in and be like everyone around us. We allow the garbage of our lives to block the light.

I want to offer a challenge to myself as well as to you. I want to spend as much time on my heart and mind as I do on my physical self. If we can find time in the day to take a shower, brush our teeth, and clean ourselves, then we can find the time to read our Bibles, pray, and clean our hearts and minds. If we are careful not to eat contaminated food and drink clean water, should we not also be careful what we take in with our hearts, mind, and eyes?

The challenge is to take care of our spiritual health and hygiene as much as our physical. To get rid of the garbage we allow to shine in our lives and allow the light of Christ, our Rock and our Hope, to shine through us.

37 - My Children are Colorblind, and That Warms My Heart

One of the reasons we decided to move our family and Stand True to Troy, Ohio was because of our friends, the Welborns. Brent has done a lot of the artwork for Stand True, as well as the layout work for our educational materials.

Brent and his family have been huge blessings in the lives of our family. They have three beautiful children: Bennett, Johanna, and Eve. Our kids love to play with the Welborn kids and were very excited to find out that we would get to live by them.

Bryan with his first and fifth children, Kimberlee and Atticus at their favorite local cafe, Troy, Ohio, 2007

It's funny how kids don't notice things that so many adults do. They just see the Welborn kids as kids who are fun to play with. Unfortunately, not everyone sees them that way. Eve, their middle child, is adopted and also African American. You can imagine the looks they get when they're out, and Eve looks up at Amy and calls her mommy.

What is amazing is how my kids have never said a word and have not even seemed to notice anything different about Eve. They simply see a little girl who they love to play with. They don't care about the color of her skin; they just care about their friend Eve.

Why is it a young child just sees the human person without adding qualifiers or labels to separate her from other people? Why is it my children can understand that Eve is a beautiful creation of God and not care about some so-called race difference?

Little children see things so purely until adults contaminate their innocence. They understand that there is really only one race, the human race. They don't care about skin color, nationality, or anything we adults hold against each other.

It is not that kids are naive about things they shouldn't be. Kids know things, like what is the difference between right and wrong. My kids know when they have done something wrong; you can see it in their eyes.

So why can't we adults take a lesson from the innocent minds and hearts of children? Why can't we recognize the personhood of every single human, regardless of skin color, nationality, or any other difference we may have? Why is it they can look at a baby in the womb and understand she is simply a baby who is younger than other kids?

This weekend, as my kids played in the back yard with Eve and her sister and brother, I was humbled by the love and blindness that my kids had toward her. They taught me a lesson this weekend. Even though I saw Eve as the beautiful little girl she was and did not care at all about the color of her skin, I still sometimes ask myself what other people are thinking when they see her and her family.

Why should I care what other people think? Why does my mind think of questions like that? I know that someday, as my children get older and they start to pick up on the hatred and bigotry that surrounds them in this world, they will be faced with decisions about what they believe. I know I cannot shield them from everything that is wrong with this world. However, I also know I can raise them and nurture them with the truth that will help mold who they become as people.

More important than what I can do for them is what Christ can do. I know, as their father on earth, I have a duty to raise them with the love my Heavenly Father has for me. I know I have the responsibility to teach them how to see others as our neighbors, no matter who they are or what they look like. I know I have to teach them to love their neighbor as themselves, as God's Word teaches us. I know the best way to teach them is to live that way myself, and to love people in the way I want them to love people.

I thank God for the Welborns and the love they have for their children. I thank God they have shown Eve the same love that they have for their natural born children and have embraced her, the way Christ embraces us when He adopts us as His own.

We all have a duty to our fellow man to love them the way Christ loves us. We all have an opportunity to live out that love in a way that will teach the next generation there is only one race—the human race. We can let our love be as blind as a child if we look at the love Christ gives us and embrace it as our standard.

"Teacher, which is the greatest commandment in the Law?" Jesus replied: " 'Love the Lord your God with all your heart and with all your soul and with all your mind.' This is the first and greatest commandment. And the second is like it: 'Love your neighbor as yourself.' All the Law and the Prophets hang on these two commandments" (Matthew 22:36-40, NIV).

38 - Everyday Opportunities

Sometimes I forget what I am wearing and wonder why people are looking at me with such strange looks on their faces. Sometimes they smile and nod at me like they know me, and other times they look like they want to strangle me.

This morning I was at the gym and noticed a women looking at me. I realized she was reading my shirt. I was wearing our "01-22-73 Silenced" shirt. She asked me what the date on my shirt was. I told her it was the date that the Supreme Court decided children in their mothers' wombs were not full human persons, and since that day we lose over 4,000 little babies each day to surgical abortion. She said she never realized it was that many and smiled at me as she continued with her workout.

I am not sure what exactly she was thinking, but I know she was thinking about what I told her. The shirt had done its job. It provoked thought and conversation. We actually try and design our shirts for that specific purpose. We don't want just to scream a message, but actually get people talking and thinking.

I was also asked by two of the gym staff this week about what church I go to. Just out of the blue, they walked up to me and asked about going to church. I make it a point to wear either a Stand True shirt or a One Truth shirt (OneTruth.com) every day to the gym. I had never talked to these two trainers about church, but they knew I was someone they could ask about it.

Now, I know this may seem like just an elaborate advertising plan to get you to buy our T-shirts, but it's not. I strongly believe in using every opportunity we have to advance the Gospel of Christ and the message of life. It is not always easy just to walk up to someone and share with them, but it is very easy to make yourself known and available for them to approach you.

Here is where I may offend some of you, and I look forward to reading the angry e-mails I'll get back for this next statement. I do not believe that every so-called Christian T-shirt is great for spreading the message. I am talking about the hundreds of rip-off shirts that just turn a company's logo into a "Christian" message.

If you go to summer music festivals, you know what I am

talking about. Instead of "Reeses" it says, "Jesus" drawn in the same way. Instead of "Budweiser" it says, "Bewiser." Instead of "Jack Daniel's" it says, "Book of Daniel." Recently, it has gotten so bad that there is a "Mountain Dew" rip-off that says, "Do the Jew." What's next, instead of "Wonder Bra" it will say "Wonder God: He'll embrace and lift you up"?

Our God is the Creator of the universe. He is our inspiration. Why is it that we cannot be creative and draw from Him for ideas and art? Why do we just rip off other art and logos? I know God has used these shirts for good, and many of you may have stories about how you were able to witness with them, but God can and will use all situations. I am simply asking if these are truly honoring to God.

There are, however, many companies out there that make some great original, thought and conversational provoking art from companies like: One Truth, No One Underground, Ephraim, Enthos, and Thorn. These companies have the same passions as we do at Stand True: to produce quality, original artwork that honors God.

I know some people may think, "What can a T-shirt or a bumper sticker really do?" You may never know what they can do or what results will come from wearing a shirt or putting a sticker on your car. Do we really need to know every result, or is it enough

Bryan being interviewed outside Planned Parenthood, Des Moines, Iowa Summer 2007

to know that the message is getting out? I met a woman once who told me a story about her trip to an abortion clinic, and how God worked.

As she drove out of her driveway to go and get an abortion, she asked God to show her a sign if He was real. She said if He showed her a sign, she would keep her baby and turn to Him. As she was about to pull into the abortion clinic parking lot a car pulled into the lane in front of her. She read the car's bumper sticker, which said, "Abortion stops a beating heart." She kept driving past the abortion clinic and is now living her life for Christ and raising a beautiful child.

We have opportunities every day that we never know about. We are around people all the time and have so many chances to witness. I would much rather wear a One Truth shirt that shows the love of Christ than a shirt that advertises some random clothing company. I would much rather wear a message promoting life than just a plain old pattern.

I challenge you to open yourself up to the opportunities in your everyday life.

39 - Christmas: A Christian Holiday or a Holiday from Christianity?

A few years ago while I drove to church with my family, we were looking at all the churches we passed on the way. We were noticing which churches were holding worship and which ones were not. This is something that is not unusual if there is a bad storm and it is too icy or snowy. However, the weather that Sunday morning was not bad, just a little rainy, yet there were several churches that remained empty and dark.

The Kemper family Christmas photo 2008: Carrie, Madilynn, Bryan, Atticus, Abigayle, Kimberlee, Jaemison, Troy, Ohio

This particular Sunday just happened also to be Christmas Day, and I was excited to have Sunday worship on Christmas. I was surprised, however, that so many churches decided to cancel worship on Christmas Day.

I enjoy spending the day with my family, watching my kids open presents, and all the other fun stuff we do on Christmas. My wife will tell you I am worse than the kids on Christmas morning. I have never in my life been able to sleep past 6:00 AM on Christmas. I love all the fun traditions as much as anyone else, but that is all they are, traditions, and they should never come before worshiping God. The whole reason we celebrate Christmas in the first place is to celebrate the birth of our Savior. How can we put presents and stockings ahead of worshiping God?

I have five children: ages eight, seven, five, three, and one, and I sat them down a couple of weeks before that Christmas to ask them a question. I told them Christmas was going to be

on a Sunday that year and asked them what was more important: church or presents? They told me church was always more
important. They did not throw any fits or get upset in the morning as we left for church, and all the presents still sat unopened
under the tree.

I guess this boils down to what is most important in our
lives. What do we truly live for? It is obvious that the business
world looks at Christmas as a gold mine with consumer frenzy
for the latest gadgets. They see dollar signs and profits and have
no problem having Christmas sales. They just won't say the
words "Merry Christmas."

When you see Christmas on TV, it is portrayed as more of a
"do-good" holiday. Get the Christmas spirit, do-good deeds, and
you will feel better about yourself. The TV programs show all
the traditions like shopping, caroling, presents, and big feasts.
You might even see a family go to a Christmas Eve service once
in a while, but don't expect to hear a true Christmas message
unless you are watching *A Charlie Brown Christmas*. I think it is
just about the only Christmas show on TV that understands the
true meaning of Christmas.

So, with the rest of the world completely in the dark about
Christmas and what it should mean, you would think that Christians and churches would be able to remain that one sane voice
during the Christmas season. I guess I should not have been
surprised when I had friends and family tell me their churches
decided to "close for Christmas." I know this should not sur-
prise me with the direction modern churches have taken lately.
I should almost expect it with churches trading in the gospel
for warm fuzzy stories. Pastors are so worried about offending
people with the truth that they have hidden it behind feel-good
services that don't have anything to do with the Word of God. So
why be shocked if the world is afraid to say, "Merry Christmas,"
when the church is afraid to proclaim the Gospel of Christ?

When you approach the Christmas season, I hope and pray
the true meaning is instilled in our children. Of course, I am
going to buy my kids some presents and have a blast opening
them on Christmas morning. If you live in Ohio, you should

drive by our house and see all the lights we have up. We love decorating for Christmas. But beyond all of the fun stuff we do for Christmas, it is primarily important that I teach my children why we are even able to have any fun at all.

I will leave you with these words from the book of Luke. This is how Linus told the story of Christmas in *A Charlie Brown Christmas*, and he nailed it.

Listen to Linus explain Christmas here: www.dltk-holidays. com/xmas/sounds/linus.wav.

And there were in the same country shepherds abiding in the field, keeping watch over their flock by night. And, lo, the angel of the Lord came upon them, and the glory of the Lord shone round about them: and they were sore afraid. And the angel said unto them, "Fear not: for, behold, I bring you good tidings of great joy, which shall be to all people. For unto you is born this day in the city of David a Saviour, which is Christ the Lord. And this shall be a sign unto you; Ye shall find the babe wrapped in swaddling clothes, lying in a manger." And suddenly there was with the angel a multitude of the heavenly host praising God, and saying, "Glory to God in the highest, and on earth peace, good will toward men" (Luke 2:8-14, KJV).

40 – Tragedy on Tour Brings New Strength and Resolve

In the summer of 2007 we had a rough second half of the Stand True Summer Mission Trip. While at Lifest in Oshkosh, Wisconsin, two of our team members witnessed a young girl as she fell off a bungee ride and died. This happened about 100 feet from our booth and really affected the team, as some of our people were planning on riding the amusement later that day.

Tour team 2007 hanging out in Philadelphia, Summer 2007

A week after this happened we were driving back from Philadelphia when we received a phone call from one of our West Coast team members. Sarah and her sister Becca were scheduled to leave for the West Coast in a couple of days, and I thought she was just checking on her flight information. She informed me that Becca's fiancée Jimmy and her friend Sonny were in a car accident that morning, and Jimmy was killed. Jimmy was a Marine and had just gotten back from serving our country in Iraq.

I pulled the van over to the side of the turnpike and just wept my eyes out. I could not believe what was going on. I tried to convince myself that it was all some sick joke and not really happening. I asked my friend Emma, Stand True's photographer, to take over driving so I could calm down and collect my thoughts.

God has really shown me so much from what happened that summer. The one thing He continually reminds me of every day is tomorrow is not promised, and I need to decide what I am going to do with today.

I have been thinking about the Bible verse I have tattooed on my arm, Psalm 40:2 (KJV), "He brought me up also out of an horrible pit, out of the miry clay, and set my feet upon a rock, and established my goings." God has lifted me out of a life that was vile and destructive and has given me the Rock, Christ, to stand on. He has washed me clean of that vile miry clay and given me eternal life with Him.

We are never guaranteed to wake up each morning, to have another day on this earth. But when we do wake up each morning, what is it we are going to live for that day? What is it that is going to inspire us to get out of bed and face the day?

As I have been praying about all that went on that summer, these are the questions I keep asking myself. I began to be really aware that each new day that I wake up and breathe the air, I have another opportunity to serve the One who created that air, who gave me the power to breathe. I have another chance to share with a dying world, a world of people who are living in that pit of destruction, of miry clay. A world that needs so badly for God's people to lay down their own selfish desires and love people the way Christ loved us.

Each day we wake up is another day to worship and enjoy our Savior, another day to learn more about Him and rest in Him. Each day we wake up is another day to cry out to Him and glorify Him. Each day we wake up is given to us by Him, and we must live that day for His Glory, to advance His Kingdom.

As I stood at Jimmy's funeral and watched his loved ones mourn his death and celebrate his new life with our Savior, I thought about my funeral. I asked myself, if I were to pass away tomorrow, would I have lived that day for the purpose in which it was given to me? I was ready to ask myself each and every day until the day I go home, what is my purpose for getting out of bed today?

41 – America Is Not a Christian Nation

This commentary may offend or upset some of you. It is not my intention to upset or offend, just to challenge you to think and examine our nation's attitude.

I was driving to church recently and listening to my wife's southern gospel radio show. A song was playing

Prayer outside abortion mill New York City, Summer 2007

about how much of a shame it is that people are trying to take God out of schools and off our money and out of the Pledge of Allegiance. I began to think about these things and actually started to feel that I did not care if God was taken out of these things.

I know this may be a shock, but I really am not concerned with God being listed on our money. In fact, I am almost in agreement that His holy name should be removed from our money. The line "In God we trust" is really a lie for most people using the money. It is a lie for our nation to have that line on the money when we do not trust in God in the reality of living.

I have noticed this Christmas season how flippantly television shows throw around the name of Jesus, like it is just any other name. What is happening is they are using God's name in vain and breaking the third commandment. Exodus 20:7 (KJV) says, "Thou shalt not take the name of the LORD thy God in vain; for the LORD will not hold him guiltless that taketh his name in vain." Taking God's name in vain is not just using it as a curse. It is using it any time when we don't really mean it. If someone says, "Thank God," and does not truly mean it, that person is using His name in vain.

When we see someone like Christina Aguilera singing disgusting songs one night and beautiful Christmas hymns another night, it is obvious she does not truly understand or believe what she is singing. The world has such a warped sense of God and what Christianity is. Christianity is not a nationality; it is not imparted to us because we were born in America. We are not born Christians. It is not something you can just call yourself expecting to reap the benefits of what it truly means to be saved. I love the old saying, "Going to church does not make you a Christian any more than going to McDonald's makes you a hamburger."

So many times I hear people say how great it is when some musician thanks God at an awards show, even though they are winning an award for a song that mocks God's law and Christianity. Or an actor thanks God for an award for a movie that is vile and disgusting. I would say they are using God's name in vain; and as the commandment says, the Lord will not hold them guiltless for taking His name in vain.

Being an American does not automatically mean you can claim Christianity. Nationality has nothing to do with Christianity, and in all reality most of our nation mocks Christianity. It is simply a label people wear that means nothing to them.

Having "In God we trust" on our money is not going to save us. Saying "One nation under God" does not make us Christian. In fact, when it is said and not meant, it is a sin and the breaking of a commandment by God.

So I say let America stop pretending to be something it is not. Let's not let people think they are OK in God's eyes just because of empty words or thanks. Singing a hymn is not going to get you into heaven, and we should not let people think it will. Having God's name on our money will not protect our country. These things are just false securities and will do nothing to save anyone.

Instead of worrying about keeping some empty words in the Pledge of Allegiance, let's give this country what it really needs, the Gospel of Christ.

Just something to think about.

42 - Chastity is for Lovers: The Difference Between Chastity and Abstinence

We are often asked why we use the word *chastity* over the word *abstinence*. Isn't it the same thing? Why would you tell married people to practice chastity? Are you saying sex is bad even if you're married?

Most people think abstinence and chastity are the same thing. Far from it. Abstinence is simply abstaining from sex, but with some people that definition becomes very fuzzy. Some would say that remaining abstinent means refraining from all sexual activity, while others would say it simply refers to sexual intercourse and nothing else.

Chastity, on the other hand, is not just about abstaining from sexual behavior; it's a lifestyle we choose to live. While chastity does include refraining from sexual activity before marriage, it also encompasses so much more.

Chastity is not just for non-married people. It's something for everyone to embrace and practice. As a married man, I must live a chaste life in my marriage and remain chaste to my wife. That does not mean that I abstain from sex with my wife. It means that I abstain from outside sexual behavior. A married couple enters into a bond and covenant with God to remain faithful to each other and to keep their marriage bed sacred

Outside of the marriage covenant, sexual behavior is simply an act of lust. While many may say they love each other and their relationship is based on love, it really cannot be defined as love. God is the creator of sex, and He made us sexual beings. However, He did set guidelines for sex and created it for a purpose.

Sex is not simply about physical pleasure, as today's society may teach. If you look at what the media, educational system, Planned Parenthood, MTV, and most of popular culture push onto the youth, you would think humans were wild animals with no self-control.

Sex is so much more than just physical pleasure. It was created for two purposes: reproduction and unity between a man and his wife. We, of course, know that there is physical pleasure involved, but that does not mean it's good for all occasions.

There is a popular saying: "If it feels good, it must be okay." We know it would be ridiculous to apply that to everything in life. I know drugs feel good, but does that make them okay? When someone commits a crime they may get a rush of adrenaline that feels good, but does that make it okay? There are many things in life that are fun and give us pleasure. That does not necessarily make them right.

Many also teach that sex is a taboo or dirty thing. While outside of the marriage covenant, sex is forbidden by God. It's not in and of itself dirty or taboo. Sex is a beautiful act that God created for man and wife to enjoy and to bring them closer together as one. Sex brings a unity and bond to a man and a woman that God intended for us to share in a loving relationship.

The word *love* is so misused in today's society. It has almost no meaning in most instances. God created love and gave us the ability to love. Lust, which is what takes place when we abuse sex and ignore its purpose, can very often be mistaken for love.

Bryan outside MTV Studios Times Square, protesting, New York City, Summer 2007

When people enter into a sexual relationship outside of the bonds of marriage, it is simply to fulfill their own selfish desires for physical pleasure. When a man pressures a woman into sex and tells her, "You would if you loved me," he is simply coercing her for his own selfish desire. Lust becomes the driving factor, not love.

When young people start to date and become physically involved, certain things happen inside their bodies. It's how we are created. Physical activity will trigger our bodies to react in ways that God intended, but He intended those reactions for marriage.

So, where do we draw the line? What is appropriate behavior for a man and woman who are not married? The question should not be, "How far can we go before it's a sin?" The question should be, "Are we acting in lust or in love?"

It seems we often just want to fulfill our own desires instead of wanting to honor God and our bodies in the way God intended. We look at sex and physical pleasure as simply that: pleasure.

Many groups teach it's unhealthy to restrain ourselves and deny sexual desires we have for each other. This comes from the mindset we should indulge in what feels good and live our lives for ourselves. This is contrary to all God teaches us about life. The scripture teaches us in Galatians 2:20 (NIV), "I have been crucified with Christ; it is no longer I who live, but Christ lives in me; and the life which I now live in the flesh I live by faith in the Son of God, who loved me and gave Himself for me."

We must live our lives for Christ and not for ourselves or for our selfish desires. Many of us forget this principle when it comes to our physical relationships, but truly unhealthy behavior is living our lives for ourselves, including engaging in sexual activity outside of the covenant of marriage. We all know many pitfalls come from promiscuous sexual behavior, such as STD's, unwed pregnancies, heartbreak, and brokenness. The world seems to try so hard to come up with false hope and protection from these dangers, but the answer is simple.

If we truly act in love and treat sex as it was intended, then we can avoid these dangers along with a need for false safety nets. If we truly act in love, we can experience sex in the way God intended it, which is the most beautiful expression of our love to each other.

If we are acting in lust, not love, then we are robbing ourselves of the true purpose of an amazing gift God gave to us. If we are acting in love, then we are honoring God and each other. If we are acting in love, we are living a chaste life both before and in our marriage.

Chastity is for lovers.

43 - What Will People Say About You?

I have not been able to get the sermon from church out of my mind all week, which is really a good thing. My pastor preached on Philippians 1:21 (NIV): "For me, to live is Christ, and to die is gain." I really can't get that verse out of my mind. It is so profound.

Bryan backstage, Cool Hand Luke concert, Cornerstone Festival, Illinois, 2006

Anyone who knows me knows I am a huge Green Bay Packers fan. I always wore my Brett Favre jersey whenever the Packers were playing. Such was the case as I sat down for a great Monday Night Football match-up between the Packers and the Rams. This was not just any ordinary Monday night game. This was Brett's 200th consecutive start, which is a major feat.

Throughout the game there was a lot of talk about what Brett has accomplished, and what kind of a guy he is. They talked a lot about how he is dealing with his wife's cancer, how he spends time with Make a Wish Foundation kids and just what an all around great guy he is. He is married to his high school sweetheart; he is an amazing father and husband; and he is one of the greatest football players of all time. They always talk about how amazing his football feats are, how no one can pass like Brett, no one loves football like Brett, or how he simply lives for football.

Now, I love Brett Favre, and, from what I have heard, he is a Christian, but that is not what I heard about last night. From what the announcers were saying, you would think for Brett, to live is football. I am not saying this is the truth in his case, but that is what he is probably going to be remembered for. That is so unfortunate.

I really sat thinking about my kids, the people I work with, and all the people who follow Stand True and the work we do. I thought about some of the cool things I have accomplished in my life and things people know me for. I asked myself, what do I live for? Do I live for Stand True? Do I live for traveling around the country, giving speeches and doing pro-life work? Or do I live for Christ? If there were TV announcers talking about my life, what would they say?

For years my friends and people I know through work have referred to me as many things. I can't tell you how many times I would walk through a concert or festival in the past and hear people say, "Hey, that was the Rock For Life Guy." People would refer to me as the "Pro-Life Guy." I was known as the guy who was on Politically Incorrect, or the guy they saw on TVU. None of these things are bad things, especially if God uses them to reach people.

I began to look at my work with Stand True and how important it is that we put Christ first in what we are doing. I don't want it to ever be said "for Bryan to live is pro-life." That would be worthless to me. I know I am called to do pro-life work, but that work must be Christ-centered.

The pro-life message is not a message about scientific facts and taking a stand against procedures. The pro-life message is not just "compatible" with Christ; it is absolutely, 100% dependent on the truth and Gospel of Christ. Christ is the foundation of everything, and if we try to build on any other foundation, we will fail. God is the creator of every single life, and He gives every human person a soul, which is why abortion is wrong. It is wrong because we are destroying God's precious life, His heritage.

The pro-life message must contain the Gospel of Christ, because that is where life truly comes from. We can stop a woman from having an abortion, but what about her soul? We can save a baby's life, but what about his soul? What good are all our efforts, if they are not grounded and centered on the truth? In all honesty, we will never save a single life, Christ will. We will never save a single baby, God will. In all we do, we are able to do it because of Christ.

"For me, to live is Christ." Wow, what a powerful and demanding verse. Like I said, I cannot get that verse out of my mind, and I hope I never do. If, for some odd reason, there is ever a highlight reel on my life like I saw for Brett, I hope it ends with one thing, "For Bryan, to live was Christ." When people talk about Stand True, I pray they say, "For Christ they stood."

CLOSING
When We Can' t See the Results of Our Work

I often hear people talk about the results of their work in ministry—how many children were fed, how many homes were built, how many items were distributed. It is great when you can show how everyone's time and money is helping. It is always encouraging, and it helps keep people interested in your work.

Things are often different in pro-life work. You really don't get to see a lot of the results for your work. Many times you are just giving out information and praying people will take it to heart. You really have to learn to trust God to be in charge of the results and know your work is changing lives, whether you see it or not.

In pro-life work so many people get frustrated because they cannot see the outcome of the work and time they invest. I have seen many people drop out because they feel they are not accomplishing anything. It is easy to stand in a soup kitchen, hand a homeless man a plate of hot food, and feel good about what you are doing. When you see his face light up as he gets a hot meal it can really make you feel good about giving your time. If we are standing in front of an abortion clinic praying, and you don't see anyone turning away, it can be spiritually and emotionally draining.

If we are just looking at the results that we see, we are looking at our work in the wrong way. God is ultimately in charge of all our efforts. He is the One who brings results. I know I have to remind myself often that I am being obedient to the Word by doing the work I do, and I have to keep myself from worrying about the results of it as much. Yes, it is important to know we are being diligent with our time and efforts, but following God's will is always right.

There are, however, times when God has shown me just how much my actions count. I remember one Sunday afternoon in California; I was standing outside an abortion clinic praying when a young woman walked up. She came over to me and another man and showed us her beautiful baby. She then told us she was driving to that very clinic months earlier to have an abortion. When she drove up, she saw us praying, changed her mind on the spot, and drove off. We never knew about this until that day. She thanked us for being there and saving the life of her baby. Since then, that has happened to me several more times, and I have heard many other similar testimonies. That one little baby would make every second I have ever spent doing pro-life work worth it. Thank God I have gotten to see so many other great fruits of this work.

I would love to be able to give you a list of just how many babies God has saved through our work. It would be amazing to report on how many lives were changed, and how many young women were spared the trauma of having an abortion or healed through Christ after they sought out forgiveness. It would probably do wonders for our fundraising if we could show our donors all the amazing things God has done though this ministry.

Bryan putting new tire on the trailer, New Hampshire, Summer 2006

While I can't give you those numbers or statistics, I can tell you we are 100% committed to this work. Even if we never get to meet another girl who changed her mind because of our work, we know it is happening, and God will continue to use us. We know it is not us who saves babies and touches lives, but God. He just uses us and gives us the opportunities to reach out in His name.

With all of this said, God is always giving us encouragement at just the right time. As I was writing this, we received a message from a young woman who told us she was able to use our website to convince her best friend not to have an abortion. God's timing is perfect.

Remember, God is ultimately responsible for the results of our work. We must always remember where our strength comes from and why we are able to do His work. When we look at it that way, we can more easily trust in God for all the results.

Just follow His Word, and He will do the rest.

An Intern's Essay
by Kate Bryan

Four years ago, my life was changed. It was touched. I was moved. I witnessed a life being saved in a way that I never thought possible. But, God is amazing and is without limitations.

From a very young age I was involved in the pro-life movement. My mother was passionately pro-life and thus incorporated us into her pro-life outreach literally since birth. We were always organizing lemonade stands for the local Right to Life branch and working the pro-life booth at the local county fairs and countless other events. I loved being involved in the pro-life movement, as abortion was a veritable holocaust in my eyes. It was unsettling to me that I myself could've been aborted, killed in the safety of my mother's womb, had my parents decided differently on accepting my existence. I was always touched by their passion for life and their choice to let my siblings and me live.

As a freshman at Ave Maria College in Ypsilanti, Michigan, I became the president of Students for Life. This opened my eyes to many aspects of the pro-life movement that I had never experienced, and it furthered my involvement. It was during my time there that I came in contact with Bryan Kemper. I remember seeing him speak at a few conferences before, but I didn't have the chance to get to know him until he came to speak at Ave Maria. When he came to speak, I was in charge of "chauffeuring" him around to all of his events. It was through this time that I became interested in working with Stand True and ended up taking part in its Summer Tour a year later. This is where the story really begins…

In the summer of 2005, I embarked on one of the hardest, most amazing, and coolest experiences of my life. Each summer, Stand True offers the opportunity for young people of high school and college age to participate in Summer Tour. It is a pro-life road trip around the U.S., where the group stops at Christian music festivals and sets up a booth, in order to reach out to the participants of the festival, and to speak with them about a plethora of moral issues, including abortion and chastity. It is an amazing witness to the gospel of life as we are present at the festivals willingly discussing whatever is on each person's heart. I am a changed person because of my summer with Stand True. My prayer during the road trip was that God would form me more fully and completely.

I drove out to Virginia to meet up with the group. We hit it off instantly, and despite a few bumps in the road, we were all inseparable. It's astounding how a group of people, who are completely different in personality and upbringing, can join together in our fight for the unborn. We spent days and nights at the music festivals, minding the booth and attending some wild concerts. It was exhausting and energizing; I was going with the flow and loving every moment. Although this was rough at times, I had no idea how intense my life was about to get.

On July 2nd, 2005, Johnny walked into my life. I remember him, his strange haircut and the intensity in his eyes. I was standing in the booth where all of the pro-life leaflets were, as well as a book that contained graphic abortion images that could be viewed only upon request. I remember Johnny just standing and looking intently at each of the leaflets. Finally, I introduced myself to him. I could see that he had something really intense on his heart, but I wanted to be compassionate and didn't want to press him to talk about anything he didn't feel comfortable discussing with a stranger.

After a few minutes of conversation, Johnny asked to see the abortion book. He took his time looking through each page, taking in every bit of the imagery photographed in the pages. Then, he looked down and saw the plastic model of the ten-week-old unborn baby. Johnny held the little baby in his hands and looked up at me and said, "Is this really what a ten-week-old baby in the womb looks like?" I looked at him and replied, "Yes." I then went on to tell him how a baby's heart is already beating at this stage, and his or her little brain is working.

He didn't say anything. He just looked at me and looked as though he saw a ghost. I asked him if everything was okay. He looked at me with tear-filled eyes and said that his girlfriend was scheduled to get an abortion, and the baby was already five months along.

I quickly told my Stand True team members at the table that I had to step away from the table for a bit. At this point, I had no idea who this "Johnny" kid was, so I told them that if I didn't come back in a few hours, to come look for me. Johnny and I stepped away from all of the tables that other groups had set up and stepped outside of the tent. We walked for a little while and then ended up finding a spot to sit down. We sat there for a couple of hours; Johnny told me about his girlfriend, how they'd met, and how they'd fallen in love. He told me about his life, his hopes, and his aspirations. Then, he spoke to me about how his girlfriend was pregnant and was scheduled to have this abortion. He felt helpless (since he was the man and he felt like she, as a woman, was going to do whatever she wanted).

As he spoke to me, I felt the pain that he was suffering, and the more he spoke the more my body became numb and my eyes filled with tears. I remember praying at that moment for the grace of God to lead me in His ways, and I prayed that I would say something of some consequence. I had sidewalk counseled outside of abortion clinics, but I was usually speaking with women, so it was a completely foreign scenario for me to be speaking with the man in this situation.

I took a deep breath and began speaking. I still don't remember exactly what I said that day, but I just let God work through me. I opened myself up, in hopes that I might say exactly what Johnny needed to hear. I had ransacked the whole booth prior to leaving and grabbed every single leaflet, book, and item that I could find. As I spoke, I gave Johnny every leaflet I had. I had everything from fetal development to post-abortive support, from medical reasoning against abortion to parenting guides, from a Bible to political literature. I had every topic imaginable covered. I had a sort of "leaflet Tourette's," if you will. I remember speaking, and Johnny so intensely listening to every word I said. I told him everything I knew about faith, life, and abortion. I explained to him that as the man in this situation, he is the father of this child and has just as much right as his girlfriend to have an opinion and to have it be taken into consideration.

After a few hours of our discussing the little life growing inside his girlfriend and every other topic known to man, we finally said goodbye. He went back to the festival, and I returned back to the Stand True booth. Upon arriving back at the booth, I broke down and cried. I was so distraught over everything that Johnny was dealing with, and I was praying that I had said something of importance to him on the situation. I went and found Bryan right away and told him everything that happened. That night and the days following, the Stand True team offered countless prayers for Johnny and his newly formed little family. I figured I would never see him again, and I put my trust in God's grace in this situation.

The days went on at Cornerstone Music Festival. But, Johnny and our conversation were constantly on my mind. On the last night of the festival, we began cleaning up our booth and packing everything up to move on to our next music festival destination. The festival was coming to an end and I couldn't help but ponder on my whole Cornerstone experience and how Johnny had become such a huge part of it. In that moment I said a little prayer for him and asked God to protect him as he travelled back home and embarked on whatever journey his life was about to take.

Just then I looked up from the box I was packing and my faux-hawk friend was standing there. "Johnny!" I exclaimed. He said he was just stopping by to say goodbye and wondered if we could go outside and talk for a few minutes. "Of course," I said. We stepped outside, and I told him about the shows I had seen and my favorite parts of the festival. I asked him the same thing, and he said, "Actually, Karen. I didn't make it to many of the shows. After we talked a few days ago, I went back to my campsite and read through everything you gave me. I've been thinking a whole lot and even called my girlfriend and told her everything you and I had talked about and everything I read in the brochures you gave me."

I stared at him with complete and utter amazement.

I couldn't believe that he missed all of the festival just to read pro-life literature and think about "what we had talked about." He went on to say that after a few really long discussions with his girlfriend, they decided to keep the baby! I nearly broke down and cried there. I gave Johnny the biggest hug ever and told him that I would support them in any way that I could and so would Stand True. I was able to exchange information at this point with Johnny, and he promised he'd be in touch soon.

I ran back to the Stand True booth and was literally jumping up and down. I told everyone the amazing news. God saved this little baby's life! It was a beautiful celebration of life. From that day on, Johnny called me quite often. The decision to keep the baby was by no means easy for them; and it actually proved to be quite the intense journey in preparation for the baby to come. But, God works through all things. He works through our struggles, through our joys, through our suffering, and through our tremendous happiness. God is always good.

On November 22nd, 2005, little baby Benjamin James was born. Although I have never met little Ben, he has remained a huge part of my life. I call him my "spiritual baby." Johnny and his girlfriend never worked out, but they continue to share custody of their beautiful baby boy, and they can't imagine life without him. Ben is now nearly four-years-old and full of joy, wonder, and awe. God granted this little family a most beautiful blessing.

Looking back on my summer with Stand True, I am nothing but honored and blessed to have had the opportunity. I never would have become friends with the people that God put in my life that summer, and I never would've experienced all of the moments of wonder and awe that God produced. Of all of the things that I witnessed that summer, I am steadfast in saying that watching God save the life of little baby Ben right in front of my eyes was the most intrinsically mind-blowing of all.

The foundation on which Stand True is built upon is Christ, which I believe to be the reason why it is so successful in its ministry. I also believe this is why God called Stand True and me to witness to Johnny on that beautiful summer day as Christ

saved baby Ben. Stand True is a humble and truth-filled organization, as it focuses on sharing the love of Christ and his
compassion to the "music festival world." I don't know what
would've happened to Johnny or little Ben if Stand True hadn't
had a booth at Cornerstone that summer. But instead, I am
comforted in knowing that Stand True continues to reach out to
countless people who never would've have heard the pro-life
message without this ministry.

The people who attend these Christian music festivals are
from all walks of life, ages, and backgrounds. Stand True trains
its team of young people and gives them all of the resources they
could possibly need, in order for them to witness to any person,
at any time, and in any place; but, above all, they focus on the
majesty of God and how He never leaves us, especially in situations when we are battling for the lives of the youngest and most
pure of His creation—babies.

Stand True was with me on the day baby Ben was saved, but
above all, God was with me. God never fails…

*"Cast your cares on the Lord, and he will sustain you; he
will never let the righteous fall."* Psalm 55:22 (NIV)

About the Statistics and Quotes

Explanation on the Numbers of Abortions

Most organizations get their information from The Alan Guttmacher Institute. While the numbers have varied from between 3,300 – 4,400 over the years, I believe that many abortion mills do not report accurate numbers. With the rise in chemical abortions in recent years I believe the *estimate* of almost 4,000 a day that I quote in this book is still low. While the number of pregnancies ending in abortion was recently reported at 22% per year, over all since 1973 the abortion rate averages at 33% or 1/3 of all pregnancies ended in abortion in the last three decades.

In 2005, the Alan Guttmacher Institute reported the following numbers:

•Nearly half of pregnancies among American women are unintended, and 4 in 10 of these are terminated by abortion. 22% of all pregnancies (excluding miscarriages) end in abortion.

•40% of pregnancies among Caucasians, 69% among Blacks, and 54% among Hispanics are unintended.

•1.21 million abortions were performed, down from 1.31 million in 2000. From 1973 through 2005, more than 45 million legal abortions occurred.

•Each year, about two percent of women aged 15-44 have an abortion; 47% of them have had at least one previous abortion.

•At least half of American women will experience an unintended pregnancy by age 45, and, at current rates, about one-third will have had an abortion.

Alan Guttmacher Institute. *In Brief: Facts on Induced Abortion In The United States*. July 2008, New York, NY: accessed Friday December 4, 2009 1:12PM. <http://www.guttmacher.org/pubs/fb_induced_abortion.pdf>

Explanations for Quotes and Sources

19 - Michael Vick / PETA article

Rolfe, John. Sports Illustrated. *Hunters become the game: PETA's call in wake of Vick plea plan has merit*, online resource a CNN site originally Posted: Tuesday August 21, 2007 2:20PM; Updated. Tuesday August 21, 2007 3:03PM, Accessed: Friday December 4, 2009 2:07PM. <http://sportsillustrated.cnn.com/2007/writers/john_rolfe/08/20/vick.peta/index.html>

PETA. *Ask the NFL to Make Class on Empathy for Animals Mandatory*, online action center Accessed Friday December 4, 2009 2:14PM. <https://secure.peta.org/site/Advocacy?cmd=display&page=UserAction&id=645>

Regarding the PETA quote, "Bellowing for strong action on behalf of dogs" - While I cannot find the original quote here is a list of twenty-six Web sources quoting my original article, including an entry as a "Yahoo Answer," DemocraticUnderground.com, LifeNews.com, and a response from an animals rights group at NewsVine.com.

<http://www.google.com/search?hl=en&q=%E2%80%9Cbellowing+for+strong+action+on+behalf+of+dogs.%E2%80%9D&start=0&sa=N&filter=0>

21 - Will Our Passion Turn Back to Apathy After the Election?

United States Department of Justice, Civil Rights Division, *Freedom of Access to Clinics Entrances (FACE) Act*, Statute 18 U.S.C. § 248, accessed online December 4, 2009 3:05PM. <http://www.justice.gov/crt/split/facestat.php>

22 - The Cover Up of Child Rape

Regarding the "Choice on Earth Cards" produced by Planned Parenthood—while they are not still available, Here is a link to a picture of the cards accessed Friday December 4, 2009 2:23PM. <http://www.jillstanek.com/archives/2007/12/post_51.html>

These are links to stories mentioning the gift certificates and holiday cards.

Bream, Shannon. Fox News, *Planned Parenthood Gift Certificates Could Be Used for Deadly Purposes*, online resource Posted: Thursday December 4, 2008; accessed Friday December 4, 2009 2:28PM.
<http://www.google.com/url?sa=t&source=web&ct=res&cd=30&ved=0CCgQFjAJOBQ&url=http%3A%2F%2Fwww.foxnews.com%2Fstory%2F0%2C2933%2C462127%2C00.html&ei=GlwZS4G8K5KklAeAkejmAg&usg=AFQjCNFg43kXb-gsCtT4sDI-jpEZ6HzQKNA>

Loughlin, Sean. CNN Washington Bureau, *No peace over Planned Parenthood's holiday card,* online resource Posted: Tuesday, December 3, 2002 6:02PM EST (2302 GMT); accessed Friday December 4, 2009 2:30PM. <http://archives.cnn.com/2002/ALLPOLITICS/12/03/abortion.christmas/>

About Bryan Kemper

Bryan Kemper is the founder and president of Stand True Ministries, a Christ-centered pro-life group determined to awaken the youth of this country and share the message of life and the Gospel of Christ.

In 1987, Bryan started his work in the Christian music industry. He was determined to be a rock star, to stand on a stage and share his testimony between songs, but God had other plans. In 1993, Bryan combined his passion for music and pro-life into one organization, Rock For Life.

Since then, Bryan has stood on many stages and shared his testimony with a variety of audiences both here in the States and internationally. A passionate and compelling orator, he has spoken at high schools and universities around the world, including Harvard, Princeton, Notre Dame, Queens University in Northern Ireland, and Cardiff University in Wales. He has taken the pro-life message to countries like Ireland, Australia, Scotland, and Austria. In the past, he has appeared as a guest on the syndicated television show Politically-Incorrect with Bill Maher and co-hosted his own call-in cable show in Portland, Oregon. Bryan has been featured on MTV, radio shows, newspapers, and magazines including the cover of the *New York Times* and a six-page layout in Swing Generation. He has also been featured in three documentary movies.

Aside from his speaking, Bryan also writes. His articles have appeared in many magazines and pro-life publications. He also used to be a beat poet in a group called Poetic Justice. His poems and songs are mostly centered on the issue of pro-life and, like everything else he does, are full of passion. Bryan Kemper has spent years reaching out to youth and encouraging this generation to get involved, and now he has endeavored to continue that outreach with Stand True Ministries. Stand True is an organization that believes the only way to stop abortion is to call out to Jesus and share His love with the nation. It is an organization that asks of young people, "Will you stand?" Bryan has certainly chosen to, and he can only hope and pray that others will too.

About Stand True

Stand True exists first and foremost to glorify God. Through the grace of God, we stand for the protection of human life from the moment of fertilization to natural death. Abortion is the act of killing a human person, and it is always wrong without exceptions.

Stand True is committed to establishing a culture of life and bringing light to a generation covered by darkness. We believe that the only true way to end abortion is to turn hearts to Christ. Though it is important for the unjust laws to change, we must first turn the hearts of our nation.

Stand True is committed to educate, equip, and activate young people to stand up and be a voice for their generation. Stand True provides resources and opportunities for this generation to stand up and be a voice for those who will never have one. With projects like the Pro-life Day of Silent Solidarity, The Stand True Summer Mission Trip, The National Mother's Day Baby Shower, and our network websites and online resources, Stand True is building a generation of leaders to help build a culture of life.

Until the silent cries of innocent children are finally heard, we will raise our voices, shine our lights. We will Stand True.

"He brought me up also out of an horrible pit, out of the miry clay, and set my feet upon a rock, and established my goings." Psalm 40:2 (KJV)

ProLifeWorld.com

T-SHIRTS, HOODIES, STICKERS, BUTTONS, PATCHES, & MORE

If you are ever harassed for your pro-life or Christian convictions, for wearing a pro-life or Christian shirt in school or any of your pro-life activism, our friends at the Alliance Defense Fund may be able to help.

Phone: 1-800-TELL-ADF
Fax: 480-444-0025
Website: www.**alliancedefensefund**.org

The Alliance Defense Fund is a legal alliance defending the right to hear and speak the Truth through strategy, training, funding, and litigation.

Feedback and Interact

1. Where do you stand on pro-life issues?

2. How will you evaluate current issues differently after reading this book?

3. Have you ever known someone who had an abortion, or who considered it? What behaviors did or could you have displayed to show your love, care, and concern for them?

4. What is your next action step(s) after reading this book?

5. Do you know someone who needs crisis pregnancy counseling? If so, you can contact Stand True Helpline at...

1-800-395-HELP (4357)

6. Do you know someone struggling with post-abortion syndrome? If so, they can contact Rachel's Vineyard at...

www.**rachelsvineyard**.org

Journal Page

Journal Page

Journal Page

Praise for

Social Justice
Begins in the Womb

"For Bryan Kemper, social justice isn't a new way to raise money, it's not a fad or a trend. Social Justice is in his DNA. Its a way of life. You're not going to want to put this book down! If you let it, it will become a part of your DNA too. It has for me."
-Ryan Dobson, President KOR Ministries

"*Social Justice Begins in the Womb* by Bryan Kemper provides the reader with an overview of the pro-life position and with effective responses to pro-abortion assertions. I am grateful to my friend Bryan for his pro-life leadership and for this contribution to a key theme: that social justice cannot be divorced from the right to life."
-Fr. Frank Pavone, National Director, Priests for Life.

"Through Bryan's writing, you will realize how important it is to never lose hope in the grace of God and how one ministry is using that grace to protect the value and dignity of our most vulnerable."
-Robert Schindler, brother of Terry Schiavo

"I encourage anyone in the belief of pro-choice to read this book. You won't find a more loving and intelectual debate on the courage it takes to choose an alternative to abortion. Absolutely impacting from life changing into life renewing.
-Jeff Gilbert, Kutless